After God's Own Heart

Worship for today as seen through the life of David

Greg Shepherd

Published in 2006 by

KEVIN MAYHEW LTD
Buxhall, Stowmarket, Suffolk, IP14 3BW
E-mail: info@kevinmayhewltd.com
www.kevinmayhew.com

9 8 7 6 5 4 3 2 1 0

ISBN 1 84417 503 0
Catalogue No. 1500869

Cover design by Angela Selfe
Edited by Barry Hart
Typeset by Richard Weaver

Contents

Acknowledgements

Special thanks to Cath – without whose support this book would never have been written.

Thanks to David Holden, Steve Cook, Barry and Colleen Hart, Matt Hosier, Terry Virgo, Alison Salvesen, the musicians and PA teams at New Community Church (past and present), Stephen Moore, Charlie and Beatrice.

Foreword

There have been many radical changes in the United Kingdom Church over the past 30 years and not least in the area of corporate worship. There have also been many books written about worship – so why another one? Surely everything that needs to be written has been written. The truth is, however, that although there have been many changes in the way we worship, mostly positive, there are growing concerns around as to whether we have 'arrived'. Are there still yet many things that we need to learn or even relearn?

Many church leaders, for example, are still grappling with contributions or lack of them in corporate worship; how much space should be given to worship leaders; and how can we ensure that our people are truly engaging with God rather than singing a few songs?

I have had the joy and privilege of working alongside Greg Shepherd as he has led our church in worship for over 20 years. His enthusiasm for pioneering in worship and his wonderfully consistent temperament (not always a trait of 'artistic people'!) has meant that our church has always flourished in the area of worship. He has exemplified the role of worship leader and his passion for God's word means that his thinking is based biblically and not under the pressure to merely conform to culture.

Based on the life and example of David, Greg has managed to bring clear teaching that helps us all to worship God in a contemporary and yet timeless way. I would recommend this book to all who long to worship God as God intended. Also to any who are concerned, as I am, that the local church is truly charismatic and not just 'trendy'; for all our musicians and worship leaders – if you will apply the truths in this book on a week-to-week basis then you will serve your church excellently and ensure that we all, from the youngest to the oldest, become a people after God's own heart.

DAVID HOLDEN

(David Holden is based at New Community Church, South East London and travels widely throughout the world as part of the Newfrontiers Core Team.)

Preface

The story of David is a compelling read. The lowly shepherd is thrust into the limelight, kills a giant and becomes king. The boy who plays his harp on the hills becomes the leader of his people, dancing before the Lord with all his might as the ark of the covenant is triumphantly returned to Jerusalem. But the life of David is not just ancient history: it has much to say to us today.

There have been many developments in the realm of church worship over the last 40 years. It is therefore essential that we search the Scriptures for principles to apply to our worship so that it remains biblical. Today's worshippers need a role model: they need look no further than David to find one.

David played anointed music that soothed Saul's troubled spirit. He led the people of God in worship when the ark of the covenant was restored. He established a large group of musicians who were highly skilled and presided over a vibrant and creative period in which worship and songwriting flourished. He is the most successful songwriter of all time; we still sing the words of his songs today, 3000 years after he wrote them.

More than this, Scripture describes David as being a man 'after God's own heart' (1 Samuel 13:14 and Acts 13:22). We have an insight into his intimate and passionate relationship with God through his psalms. These challenge and inspire us, communicating much about the God he served and showing how we, too, can be those who actively seek after the Lord.

Today's church needs men and women with the spirit of David – those who are passionate for their God and who long for true biblical worship to be restored: worship that is joyful, passionate and inspired by the Holy Sprit. Worship that is in both spirit and truth.

This book was written primarily to help those who are closely involved in church worship – musicians, worship leaders, songwriters and church leaders. However, I hope that its principles will also be useful to those who may not have these roles, but are seeking to understand more about biblical worship.

Join with me in discovering true worship through the life of David and be challenged by a man who was truly 'after God's own heart'.

CHAPTER 1

Character: Looking on the heart

It is tempting to begin a book about David by looking at his considerable gifting and achievements. But this would be the wrong place to start. God's perspective is different. Before David even comes on the scene, God defines how we should evaluate him:

> The Lord does not look at the things man looks at. Man looks at the outward appearance, but the Lord looks at the heart. *1 Samuel 16:7*

In any study of David our first priority must be to look at character. This should also be our primary criterion in the assessment that we make of musicians and worship leaders in our churches. It is easy to be drawn to people's gifting. Sometimes an individual's musical ability shines out and we are understandably tempted to give them opportunities to play and lead. With some, their ability to hear from God and to lead people in worship shows a great level of anointing, yet if their gifting is not matched by their character they, and we, will encounter problems in the future!

The first book of Samuel shows the difficulties that arise when someone leads God's people through natural abilities alone. In his outward appearance Saul was a good choice as king. He was 'a head taller than any of the others' (1 Samuel 10:23), and led Israel successfully in military campaigns – he rescued the city of Jabesh (1 Samuel 11), defeated the Philistines near Gibeah (1 Samuel 14:15-23), and won a devastating victory over the Amalekites (1 Samuel 15). Yet, as readers of 1 Samuel will know, his spiritual life was in poor condition. The pressures of leadership caused him to lose patience and offer sacrifices before Samuel arrives (1 Samuel 13:8-10). He made rash and foolish statements that nearly led to his son being put to death (1 Samuel 14:24-45). In chapter 15 he disobeys the Lord's instructions and also erects a monument to his own honour. Ministry based on gifting alone that is not supported by a solid foundation of godly character can collapse under the pressures that we inevitably encounter in leadership positions.

I am not for a moment suggesting that gifting is unimportant. David was able to lead Israel in battle because he was a mighty warrior; his songs were used by the Israelites because they were inspired compositions. David himself recognised talent in his worship team: 1 Chronicles 15:22 says that 'Kenaniah the head Levite was in charge of the singing; that was his responsibility because **he was skilful at it.**' We are unlikely to take our congregations to the heights of worship if our singers are out of tune! But it is dangerous if we do not balance our assessment of the gifting of musicians and worship leaders with an evaluation of their character.

We will therefore begin our study of David by looking at his character. While only the Lord can truly look on the heart, we can gain much insight about David from looking at the biblical accounts of his life. 1 Samuel 17, the first chapter where David plays a leading role, tells us much about him.

A godly man

David came as a servant (1 Samuel 17:17-19)
David's appearance at the battlefield did not arise from a motivation to be the people's champion. He was merely running

an errand for his father, Jesse, to take provisions to his brothers. He arrived on the scene as a servant, and ended up serving God's people in a way that he did not expect, as their leader and champion.

If our motivation is to seek glory for ourselves it is unlikely that we will find long-term success. While God uses people with mixed motives (otherwise no one would ever be used by him!), he 'opposes the proud but gives grace to the humble' (James 4:6).

When I have been thrust forward in ministry it has always been when I have not been expecting it, but have been merely trying to serve God's people. I have to confess that there have been other occasions when I have desired ministry opportunities for the prestige I believed they would bring. On these occasions I always seem to have been (rightly) passed over! I have therefore learnt the hard way not to hustle! David prayed 'Give me an undivided heart that I may fear your name' (Psalm 86:11). As we offer ourselves to the Lord, he is able to change us so that our motives become purer than before.

David was passionate about the kingdom advancing
(1 Samuel 17:26)

David is naturally interested in the reward that will be given to the successful champion, but his overriding motivation is that the armies of the living God are being defied. Are we gripped with a passion to see ground taken from the enemy? This must be our desire, rather than merely to play music or to be in leadership. I am drawn to accounts written of the great sacrifices people made during the Second World War. They were not motivated by thoughts of personal glory but by a burning desire to see good triumph over the evils of Nazism. At all times our motivation should be a desire to see the kingdom advancing and the darkness of the enemy pushed back.

David had experience of fighting (1 Samuel 17:34)

When Saul challenges David about his credentials as a fighter, David replies that he has experience of fighting, albeit in a personal setting. It is very important for worship leaders to gain as much private experience of worship as possible by setting aside times to praise the Lord on their own. It is so much easier to lead others once you are familiar with leading yourself in worship. In fact, it is difficult to lead others to places that you have not been yourself.

Over the past decade, I have found spending regular times of worship on my own the single area that has most transformed my life. I have felt God envision me, speak to me, lifting my head when I've felt downcast, or sharing my joy when things have been going well. I believe that this has not just been rewarding for its own sake, but helps me to be comfortable in leading worship – it feels 'natural' because I have been leading myself into worship. Starting off with a song or two and then being led spontaneously by the Holy Spirit in times on my own has helped me to improvise in church meetings, and not feel too uncomfortable when the worship times I've been leading have taken an unexpected direction!

It can be frustrating when we'd like to lead worship in our churches but are not chosen very often. If you're in this situation, try not to be despondent. Set aside times to worship, and you will benefit from them. As you spend time with him, you equip yourself for future days when you *are* given opportunities. You are more likely to be chosen if your devotional life with the Lord is developing, as others will notice the change in you: 'For physical training is of some value, but godliness has value for all things, holding promise for both the present life and the life to come' (1 Timothy 4:8).

David was disciplined in sharpening his skills (1 Samuel 17:49)

While looking at 1 Samuel 17:49 involves skipping a little

ahead in the story, it's worth making the point that David had obviously practised a lot with his sling. Can you imagine what might have happened if David was a bit rusty when he approached Goliath? He was not going to get time to have a few practice shots! He had to be ready.

It's important for us as worship leaders to sharpen our skills on our instruments. One time when I was worshipping on my own I felt God ask me 'Do you feel called to do this?' (i.e. play music). 'Yes Lord,' I replied. 'Why don't you practise then?' came the Lord's next question, only this time I couldn't answer! I try to make sure I'm familiar with the songs I'm using in worship. If we can play through the songs without having to think too hard about the next chord we can focus more intently on the Lord. Discipline is a necessary attribute of those involved in worship.

David was faithful (1 Samuel 17:34-35)

1 Samuel makes it clear that David was faithful in the tasks he was asked to carry out. He is diligently looking after the sheep in chapter 16 when Samuel arrives, and obeys his father in running the errand in chapter 17. Verses 34 and 35 show that he is willing to put his own life in danger in order to protect the flock that he has been entrusted with.

Most of us are unlikely to be asked to lead worship at a major conference. However, many of us will be asked to lead worship in small church gatherings, perhaps in someone's home. God is looking for those who will provide faithful and passionate commitment, like David did, even when he was away from public gaze.

When I have been approached by musicians who wish to play in the Sunday morning meetings at our church, I some-times respond by asking them to play at small meetings, to see if they are reliable before I ask them to play in the bigger setting of our main Sunday meeting. Most have been exemplary in their commitment and I have therefore been happy to move them into larger settings. However, over the years, a few have not been faithful in small things and I have not used them for higher-profile events.

David was submissive

David is a role model in the area of honouring godly authority. David submitted to the authority of his father, running the errand he was charged with and looking after his father's sheep without any hint of complaint. However, as we read through the whole story of David it is his submission to Saul that really stands out.

While David initially had reason to be thankful to Saul for giving him opportunities to show his abilities, both musically and militarily, soon the dream had become a nightmare. David's chief role became providing a target for Saul's spear-throwing practice! Yet despite this and false accusations of betrayal, David still holds an exemplary attitude of submission to Saul. Refusing a golden opportunity to kill the man who is seeking his own life, David says:

> I will not lift my hand against my master, because he is
> the Lord's anointed. *1 Samuel 24:10*

David could have taken the view that, as God had called him to be king, he could speed up the Lord's work by killing Saul. After all, wasn't this opportunity to be alone with an unsuspecting Saul given by God? Saul was on the way out as God had rejected him (see 1 Samuel 15:23) and he was less popular with the people than David (1 Samuel 21:11).

Instead, David focuses not on Saul's abilities (manifestly lacking) or the way Saul had treated David (totally unjustly), but rather on his office – his God-given authority to be king.

When we submit ourselves to church leaders we are not doing so because of their abilities (gifted though they may be) or whether they have treated us fairly or unfairly. Rather we seek to honour the office that God has ordained and to please him.

When Saul dies David executes the man who claims to have killed him, on the grounds that he has 'destroyed the Lord's anointed'. David then pays tribute to Saul (2 Samuel 1:17-27).

Why character is more important than gifting

Gifting can lead you into ministry opportunities – but with those opportunities comes pressure that will test your character.

Let's imagine that in your church you have a very gifted musician playing guitar and leading worship in small group meetings. His or her gifting is evident to all. Character issues are lurking beneath the surface; however, these have not previously emerged because there are no substantive pressures in this small setting. Due to their gifting the guitarist is asked to play in a large meeting, in a band led by someone else. Instantly this guitarist faces additional pressures:

- *Submitting to someone else.* The musician is following someone else's leading. They will need to submit to someone else's selections of songs and ideas for arrangements.

- *Fitting in with other musicians.*

- *'Event pressure'.* Everyone's keyed up for the big occasion, but the setting is unfamiliar. There may be PA problems and the musician can't hear himself/herself that well.

It is in environments such as these that we see people's true characters – not when they can do everything their own way, with few external constraints! If the foundations aren't right, cracks begin to emerge when pressure comes!

Perhaps the above example is a little simplistic. My experience is that usually for the first few occasions someone is in a bigger setting they are on their 'best behaviour' and there are no problems – these only emerge over time! But if there are weaknesses, these will eventually become evident.

David was not passive about character improvement

It can be tempting to accept wrongful attitudes and behaviours as 'personality traits' but this is unbiblical. While the power to change us lies with the Lord alone, David knew that change in character comes from seeking the Lord. In Psalm 86:11 he says:

> Teach me your way, O Lord, and I will walk in your truth;
> give me an undivided heart, that I may fear your name.

He also recognises that he is not yet even aware of some of his flaws:

> Who can discern his errors? Forgive my hidden faults.
> *Psalm 19:12*

Part of our journey with the Lord through this life involves the revelation of 'hidden faults'! Often he does this through our involvement with other people – and sometimes it is others who point out our deficiencies – which can be hard to accept! I have to admit that it is only through my involvement in church music that I have become painfully aware of areas of ungodly ambition, impatience, and irritability within me! The Holy Spirit shows us weaknesses in our characters not to crush us or condemn us but so that we might seek God to change us. The process of character change is lifelong and is often a painful experience, but is all part of God's overall goal – for us to be like Jesus.

It is essential that as musicians and worship leaders we work hard on developing our characters. Scripture exhorts us:

> Make every effort to add to your faith goodness; and to
> goodness, knowledge; and to knowledge, self-control;

and to self-control, perseverance; and to perseverance,
godliness; and to godliness, brotherly kindness; and to
brotherly kindness, love. For if you possess these qualities
in increasing measure, they will keep you from being
ineffective and unproductive in your knowledge of our
Lord Jesus Christ.   *2 Peter 1:5-8*

Ultimately, God is far more interested in whether we live
godly lives than how 'successful' we are in our music ministries.
When our life's work is tested (see 1 Corinthians 3:11-15) it
will only be those works that are truly of God that will remain.

The testing of a godly man

David is anointed in 1 Samuel 16. He has clearly been chosen
by God to become king. Shortly afterwards he finds himself
in Saul's court, then thrust into the limelight before all the
Israelite army as a clear leader of God's people. Later he marries
the king's daughter.

After this whirlwind beginning, surely it would be only a
short time before David became king? He must have thought
this would happen while he was still only a teenager! There
was no doubting that God had clearly chosen him and given
him leadership gifts, and a true godly character.

As we know, the story is not like this. David encounters
many testing situations and does not become king over Judah
until he is thirty and over all Israel until he is thirty-seven.
Even then, he still faces some major tests and trials in his life.
Yet God's hand is as much upon him during his twenty years
of waiting as it is on the battlefield with Goliath. David is
being refined so that his character, already godly, matures.

You may feel that God's calling is on your life. You know
he has chosen you to perform particular tasks. Like David, you
have experienced success already in the ministry opportunities

you have been given. Yet you feel frustrated that the things that God has promised have not yet materialised.

The time of waiting is just as important as the time of opportunities. God wants us to . . .

> . . . become mature, attaining to the whole measure of the fullness of Christ. Then we will no longer be infants, tossed back and forth by the waves, and blown here and there by every wind of teaching and by the cunning and craftiness of men in their deceitful scheming. Instead, speaking the truth in love, we will in all things grow up into him who is the Head, that is, Christ.
>
> *Ephesians 4:13-15*

God's main interest is to build our characters, not our ministries! Any ministry must be built upon a foundation of good character. Often character is refined through adversity.

God allows David to go through a period of agonising trouble: from 1 Samuel 18 to 2 Samuel 5, or twenty years!

Let us for a few moments consider the tests David went through in this period:

Other people's issues

Sometimes we can bear the brunt of other people's issues with God. When Saul is jealous of David (1 Samuel 18:6-9), some of this may be due to the fact that Saul knows that his own relationship with God is not as it should be. Sometimes when we face opposition from people it is not personal; we are bearing the brunt of areas they are struggling with.

Demonic opposition

As worship leaders we are a highly visible part of God's army. This means we can attract demonic opposition. We see in 1 Samuel 18:10-11 how Saul is not fully in control of himself – powers and principalities are at work. We can also see that

God is in control of the whole situation as he delivers David. There will be times as worship leaders and musicians when the opposition we face, sometimes from individuals, is not really initiated by flesh and blood but is from demonic forces.

The test of praise

David experiences how praise tests people in 1 Samuel 18:7: 'Saul has slain his thousands, and David his tens of thousands.' Musicians are tested by:

- *The praise they receive.* David received praise but he did not become big-headed. The fact that his praise came from members of the opposite sex would have added to the temptation, but there is no evidence that David became proud as a result of it.

- *The praise they don't receive.* Like anyone else, musicians love to feel appreciated. When we don't receive commendation it is a test.

- *The praise others receive.* We are tested when others are honoured and not ourselves. Saul was jealous of David and David would have observed the damaging effect of Saul's ungodly reaction.

God made us to desire praise, but the problem we have is that often we look for recognition from people, not from the Lord.

The test not to retaliate

Despite terrible treatment by Saul, David never retaliates. As D. F. Payne says, 'Saul was David's enemy, but David was never Saul's enemy.'*

---

* D. F. Payne, *New Bible Commentary*, IVP, 1994, p. 314.

The test of the limelight, followed by obscurity

David had fame thrust upon him, and then spent many years in obscurity. When we experience a season of ministry, followed by a lack of opportunities, this can be hard.

The test of experiencing your own weaknesses

David practises deception. He lies to Ahimelech (1 Samuel 21:2) and deceives Achish (1 Samuel 21:13 and 1 Samuel 27:10-11). He is not a role model in every area. When we experience difficulties it can expose weaknesses in our characters and we are given a painful dose of self-awareness! Our deficiencies, which were there all the time, only become apparent to everyone else once we are in a place of leadership. They are then not only public but cause consequences for others! When we realise this it can be so painful that we may feel like withdrawing from leadership! Instead of allowing it to crush him, David grew stronger for the experience. Another aspect of the story of David is that God is bigger than our weaknesses and can rescue us from the messes we get ourselves into! In 1 Samuel 29, David is almost in the position where, through his own deception, he may have to fight with the Philistines against his own people. Just in time there is a dramatic change in the situation so that David is spared fighting at all. God is good to us even though we don't deserve it!

The trials and temptations David faced kept him humble and dependent upon God. If David had really believed that through his own strength and abilities he could 'slay his tens of thousands' then, by relying on his own strength he would have put himself in a precarious position!

David learned many things during this period; for example:

How to lead a group (1 Samuel 22:1-2)

> David left Gath and escaped to the cave of Adullam.
> When his brothers and his father's household heard

> about it, they went down to him there. All those who were in distress or in debt or discontented gathered round him, and he became their leader. About four hundred men were with him.

David had a group of people around him. While he had led men on the battlefield before, this was a very different situation that required alternative skills. It may not have been the easiest group to manage.

While there were no doubt reasons why individuals were disaffected with Saul, some people always become disgruntled with whatever leadership is over them! Such people would have been a test for David, and he would have had to develop the skill to lead them. It would not have been easy to be in leadership over members of his own family, particularly if Eliab's comments in 1 Samuel 17:28 are anything to go by ('I know how conceited you are and how wicked your heart is; you came down only to watch the battle')! As part of your training for leading worship and musicians in the future, God may place you in other positions of leadership, perhaps in other aspects of church life, in order to broaden your skills and experience.

How to hear from God (1 Samuel 23:1-12)

David learnt to enquire of the Lord during this time when he was away from the king's court. While I am sure he would have sought God's counsel in the past, here the stakes are high – he is putting other men's lives at risk. It is one thing to believe that you have heard from God where no real risk is involved, quite another to change career or to move house because you sense the Lord is leading you to do so. You then run the risk that if it does not work out your family may suffer. Yet it is in these situations that we learn much that helps us in future leadership.

The value of true friendship (1 Samuel 23:16)

David benefited from the unselfish friendship of Jonathan,* who shared his possessions with David and helped him even though he was a threat to Jonathan's succession as king. When we are in times of crisis it is invaluable having others around us who help us 'find strength in God'.

How to resist challenges to leadership and find strength in God alone (1 Samuel 30:6)

When the Amalekites capture David's wives and the women and children of his men this must have been a time of the most intense pressure. Not just because of natural anxiety as to the fate of his own family, but also because it was a serious test of his leadership – 'the men were talking of stoning him; each one was bitter in spirit because of his sons and daughters. But David found strength in the Lord his God.' David appears to have no colleagues or friends to turn to, but God meets his needs and brings him through to triumph ('David recovered everything the Amalekites had taken' – 1 Samuel 30:18). An experience like this changes us within. It gives us strength and courage for the next time we face challenges.

How to resist pressure to act until God has spoken
(1 Samuel 30:7-8)

During this situation, the greatest temptation would have been for David to charge after the Amalekites – it would have been the natural thing to do. However, David waits to enquire of God before acting. This is a vital lesson for any leader to learn.

---

* There is more on Jonathan's friendship with David in Chapters 9 and 10.

How to bring unity where there was possible division
(1 Samuel 30:21-25)

Once the women and children have been safely rescued David had a further test. One-third of his 600 men had been too exhausted to continue the pursuit, which was successfully completed by the remaining 400. There were some who complained that David should not give shares of the plunder to those who had not completed the rescue. David discerns that the attitude behind the complaints is from 'evil men and trouble-makers' (verse 22). He also sets the tone for his future kingship – all should benefit equally. Furthermore, he shrewdly gives a share to the 'elders of Judah', which must have helped him to cement relationships with them – they appoint David as king long before the rest of Israel.

The waiting period was vital for David's development as a leader. A period of waiting and testing did not happen to David alone – but also to Moses, Joseph and even the Son of God, who 'learned obedience from what he suffered' (Hebrews 5:8).

The result was that when David takes up his throne:

> [He] is a man who has sufficient contentment and trust in God that he does not feel threatened by his predecessor . . . his personal ambition has been subjected to God's will. Here is a man of faith, of patience, a man without consuming personal ambition. A man prepared for kingship.*

When you go through a testing time and have to wait to receive what the Lord has promised you – please take heart: God is refining you to be the godly man or woman he made you to be! When we are waiting for ministry opportunities we can be despondent and passive, but David's life shows that God's training programme continues during this time and we

---

* Michael Eaton, *Preaching through the Bible: 2 Samuel*, Sovereign World, 1996, p. 11.

can learn many useful skills. God is more interested in our character than in our ministries. How many worship times we've played in or led, or how many songs we've written, is not important: what matters is whether we have lived as true disciples of Jesus.

Points to remember

- *God defines us through our characters, not our ministries.*
- *David arrived at the battlefield as a servant, not as a superstar!*
- *David was equipped for the public arena because he had won private battles.* Personal worship will equip us for public worship leading.
- *David was disciplined and sharpened his skills.* As musicians we need to be familiar with the songs we will play.
- *David was faithful in carrying out errands.* We may not get opportunities to be involved in large meetings, but the Lord is looking for us to be faithful in small things. These may lead to greater opportunities later.
- *David was submissive to leadership appointed by God,* regardless of the leader's failings.
- *David was not passive about character improvement* – he asked the Lord to change him, even his 'hidden faults'.
- *David went through many tests and trials* before he received what God had promised him and learned many skills during this time.
- *God is looking to develop our characters,* which may take many years.

Questions for personal application

1. Who do you know whom you believe has a godly character? How would you define their characteristics?

2. In what ways would you say that being a church musician is servanthood?

3. Are there some areas of ministry that you believe God has promised to you?

4. Have you gone through any times of trial? What were these and what do you feel you learned from them?

5. David was not passive about character improvement. What areas of your character do you believe need to change? Have you already seen God's hand at work to change you?

Additional material

Please see the character questionnaire in Appendix II as a light-hearted test of our motives and reactions.

CHAPTER 2

Worship: The overflow of the heart

'and the Lord is with him' (1 Samuel 16)

We have already seen how David possessed a godly character that provided a platform for him to be used by God. In the second half of 1 Samuel 16 we see how David demonstrated that there was an anointing upon him for ministering to others in worship.

In 1 Samuel 16:14-23 Saul, who has disobeyed the Lord, is in spiritual torment. Saul's servants suggest that, if they find a musician who can play for him, this will alleviate the king's feelings. Verse 18 says:

> One of the servants answered, 'I have seen a son of Jesse of Bethlehem who knows how to play the harp. He is a brave man and a warrior. He speaks well and is a fine-looking man. *And the Lord is with him.*'

It is notable that the servant does not confine his description of David's suitability to his musical ability and his physical characteristics. There was something else about David that set him apart from other musicians: those around him recognised that 'The Lord is with him.'

This was apparent at the end of 1 Samuel 16:23 when it says that 'Whenever the spirit from God came upon Saul, David would take his harp and play. Then relief would come to Saul; he would feel better, and the evil spirit would leave him.'

David did not just provide some soothing background music to Saul: more than this, God worked through David's playing and his grace and peace were communicated to Saul.

As we have seen in the previous chapter, good character is essential. The ability to be able to play well is also important. Psalm 33:2-3 instructs us to 'praise the Lord with the harp; to make music to him on the ten-stringed lyre. Sing to him a new song; **play skilfully**, and shout for joy.' But as musicians and worship leaders what we desire is more than this.

When we observe a gifted worship leader or an anointed musician playing we appreciate that what they have is more than just musical skill, important though this is. We see that they are able, through the Spirit of God, to exert an influence upon the congregation, assisting them in their own worship. Like David with Saul, we see that they bring about a transformation in those around them, leading others into a greater awareness of God's grace and peace.

How does this happen? Can we do anything to cultivate this in our own lives? David provides us with a few clues.

David had a special anointing, but the Lord is also with us

Earlier in 1 Samuel 16 we are told that

> Samuel took the horn of oil and anointed him [David]
> in the presence of his brothers, and from that day on the
> Spirit of the Lord came upon David in power.
>
> *1 Samuel 16:13*

David had a special calling from the Lord, to become king. None of us is ever likely to have that role, but some of us will know that the Lord has asked us to perform particular tasks for him, whether now or in the future. Like David, we will know God's empowering for these ministries when the time comes. The call of God is not something that can be manufactured, but is bestowed according to God's infinite mercy, wisdom and grace.

However, I also believe that we can *all* say that 'the Lord is with us'. The New Testament makes it clear that, like David, the Spirit of God is upon each of us in power.

> In him we were also chosen, having been predestined according to the plan of him who works out everything in conformity with the purpose of his will . . . Having believed, you were marked in him with a seal, the promised Holy Sprit, who is a deposit guaranteeing our inheritance until the redemption of those who are God's possession – to the praise of his glory. *Ephesians 1:11-14*

Under the new covenant God dwells within those who are saved. 1 Corinthians 6:19 says that our bodies are 'a temple of the Holy Spirit, who is in you'. 1 John 4:4 tells us 'the one who is in you is greater than the one who is in the world.' Therefore we can have faith that the Lord is with each of us who believes.

God gives us grace for the role we are given

Furthermore, when we are assigned particular tasks within our churches we should anticipate that the Lord will be with us to assist us. We have already seen how Saul was not the most suitable king for Israel. Yet, in line with the office he was given, Saul was empowered by God. For example, we read of the Spirit of God coming upon Saul in power in 1 Samuel 10:10 and in 1 Samuel 11:6. If we are asked to play our instrument in worship or to lead a meeting, we can claim in faith that with the appointment will come the measure of grace and empowerment from the Lord that we need. 'Let us then approach the throne of grace with confidence, so that we may receive mercy and find grace to help us in our time of need' (Hebrews 4:16).

Anointing comes through relationship

However, I believe that when Scripture says about David that 'the Lord is with him', this does not just mean an empowering that came from the Lord purely through David's calling, or through the roles he would be required to play as warrior and king. What Saul's servant could sense was David's relationship with God overflowing so that when David played the harp those around him experienced a measure of the encounters that David had with God.

Our playing in, and leading of, our church's worship times flows out of our own personal relationships with God. Natural gifts, such as proficiency in singing and the ability to lead others, assist greatly in facilitating our congregations to worship the Lord. However, these are secondary influences in worship compared to the level of relationship that each of us have with the Lord.

When we read David's psalms we are inspired: the praise he brings to God provokes us to praise the Lord also. When we read Psalm 8:1-3, 'O Lord, our Lord, how majestic is your name in all the earth . . . When I consider your heavens, the work of your fingers, the moon and the stars, which you have set in place', we cannot help but be moved to worship our Creator. When we hear the words of Psalm 145:1-2, 'I will exalt you, my God the King; I will praise your name for ever and ever. Every day I will praise you and extol your name for ever and ever', we, too, are impacted by David's praise. We read Psalm 139 and we are in wonder at God's personal knowledge of every aspect of our lives. When we look at Psalm 63 we too experience something of David's longing for his Lord. In the words of A. W. Tozer:

> David's life was a torrent of spiritual desire and his psalms ring with the cry of the seeker and the glad shout of the finder.[*]

---

[*] A. W. Tozer, *The Pursuit of God*, Kingsway, 1984, p. 16.

Even 3000 years later, our contact with David, the worshipper, through his psalms encourages us to worship. We taste something of his close relationship with the Lord, and this inspires us to worship and to long for more of our Lord.

As worship leaders and musicians, our greatest desire is to have this same characteristic that David had: to inspire those around us to worship. We long that the Lord will place something in us that flows out to our congregations that invokes worship. This might be our playing, our singing, our leading or a song we have written.

We can cultivate an anointing

We can sometimes be passive about wanting to grow in our gifting. We can believe that, like Moses, we will wait in a wilderness until the grand day of our calling when we will suddenly be thrust into the limelight and the Lord will be with us powerfully thereafter. However, the pattern we see with David is that when he emerged into the glare of Saul's court he had prepared himself. He had already developed his relationship with the Lord.

How did he do this? David's psalms provide us with some indications.

David sought after God

David was passionate in his desire for the presence of God. In Psalm 63:1 he cries out:

> O God, you are my God, earnestly I seek you; my soul
> thirsts for you, my body longs for you, in a dry and weary
> land where there is no water.

In the next verse he says 'I have seen you in the sanctuary and beheld your power and your glory.'

Surely David had already met with God if he had seen him in the sanctuary and beheld him? Yet David knew that God had called him to an ongoing relationship: not one life-changing meeting. A. W. Tozer says that salvation is 'not an end, but an inception, for now begins the glorious pursuit, the heart's happy exploration of the infinite riches of the Godhead'.* We are called to seek after him.

Before I became a Christian I thought that music was the best thing life had to offer. It seemed that music was the means to communicate every thought and feeling, and when I listened to great music I felt that this transcended ordinary existence. Then, after committing my life to Christ I can remember walking along the street and sensing the presence of God around me for the first time. I realised that he loved me, accepted me, and understood everything about me. The Lord's presence made everything else, including music, pale into insignificance. Music became secondary to seeking after the living God, who truly has 'eternal pleasures at [his] right hand' (Psalm 16:11).

Yet so often we can be inconsistent in this quest. At times we can allow other activities to compete for our devotion. Sometimes we can substitute good things, like serving his people, for the best, seeking after God. Sometimes we can seek after a spiritual experience rather than an encounter with a person.

David realised that the love of God is 'better than life' and that only through relationship with God would his 'soul be satisfied as with the richest of food'. This made David 'stay close' to God (Psalm 63:3, 5, 8).

How do we seek after God? I believe that it requires the setting aside of time to be with him. The devotion of time in the day when we are at our most alert and can communicate with him while we still have some energy left. Jesus drew aside and prayed to his Father morning and evening. No time of the day is especially sacred – you will know what is most suitable for you – but Jesus' lifestyle implies that devotions should be

---

* A. W. Tozer, *The Pursuit of God*, Kingsway, 1984, p. 14.

regular and frequent. I believe it involves coming to God to desire his presence, rather than have a 'shopping list' of things to pray for (though intercession is important too).

As we do this we will find that our knowledge of him grows. We will discover that we are changed to be more like him. Our desire for him will increase.

David communicated all his innermost thoughts and feelings to the Lord

In Psalm 139:4 David is well aware of God's omniscience: 'Before a word is on my tongue you know it completely, O Lord.' David understood that God knew everything about him: every action, every thought, every feeling. David could have taken the view that as this was the case he did not need to communicate with God. Instead, the reverse is true: David's psalms are full of his rawest emotions. He expresses joy, sorrow, anger, repentance, praise, and perplexity to his Lord. Why does he do this?

When we articulate our feelings to the Lord, we bring them into the light of his presence. We are effectively submitting them to him, and can receive his tender mercy and hear his counsel. I would encourage you, like David, to communicate your feelings to the Lord: even feelings that are not godly – the Lord is able to handle these! In admitting these we open ourselves up to the possibility of change.

David sought to abide in God's presence

David wished to be someone who was continually aware of the Lord's presence. In Psalm 27:4 he writes:

> One thing I ask of the Lord, this is what I seek:
>   that I may dwell in the house of the Lord all the days
> of my life,
>   to gaze upon the beauty of the Lord and to seek him
> in his temple.

David was aware that it is easy to spend days of our lives not 'dwelling' with the Lord: not really aware of his presence, his goodness and love towards us. To 'dwell in the house of the Lord' requires us to be active, not passive. And David is also aware that it is not enough to be in the house of the Lord, his temple: David knew he needed to focus actively upon the beauty of the Lord, to seek after him.

I believe that God's desire is not for us to have *occasional* encounters with him, followed by withdrawal, like a desert traveller occasionally refreshing himself at an oasis. Instead he wants us to be continually drinking at the well of his presence. Jesus commanded us to 'Remain in me, and I will remain in you . . . Neither can you bear fruit unless you remain in me' (John 15:4).

David was dependent upon God

Many of David's psalms demonstrate that he was dependent upon the Lord. In Psalm 3, when his life was under threat from his son Absalom's rebellion – 'many are saying of me, "God will not deliver him"' – he states, 'But you are a shield around me, O Lord; my Glorious One, who lifts up my head' (verses 2-3).

In Psalm 86:1 he cries, 'Hear, O Lord, and answer me, for I am poor and needy' and asks the Lord to guard his life.

There are many, many other examples we could choose. Often David's position was so desperate he had no choice – he knew that only God could save him. I am sure the majority of us will not face so many life-threatening situations: nevertheless an attitude of dependence upon the Lord, rather than our own strength, is a strong feature of David's life that would benefit us also. Trust in God, rather than in our own abilities, allows God room to change situations for his glory.

David enquired of the Lord

While it is good to seek God's presence for his own sake,

however, there are also times when it is very important to seek after the Lord for an answer for particular situations.

There are five occasions recorded in Scripture in which David enquired of the Lord for specific guidance.* I am sure there are many more that were not recorded.

God is pleased when we come to him to ask for answers to particular situations. This might be counsel for a life-changing decision, or it may be which songs you should use for a particular worship time. Whatever the situation, it is good to seek the Lord for the answer.

David had an understanding of God's character based on his own experience

The result of the passionate, intimate relationship David had with God is that when David sings about God's character this does not come across as just an intellectual understanding. The Psalms do not read like a theological textbook, but display an understanding of God's character *translated through a personal relationship*. For example, Psalm 139 does not provide us with a theoretical explanation of omniscience and omnipresence, but instead applies these concepts to David's day-to-day existence. God's intimate knowledge of David brings him security and leads him to worship his Creator.

David's understanding of who God is comes not just from religious teaching but through the application of it to his life – the experience of seeing God save, forgive, deliver and provide. As musicians it is good for us to study the Bible to gain as much understanding as possible of theological truth as we seek to lead congregations in worship and I recommend that you do this. However, as we spend time with the Lord we begin to express these truths from personal experience. Just as

---

* These are: 1 Samuel 23:2 and 4; 1 Samuel 28:6; 1 Samuel 30:8; 2 Samuel 2:1; and 2 Samuel 5:19.

David's psalms impact us because they are based on the reality of his experience of the Lord and his workings in his life, so our leading of our congregations will be enhanced.

In fact, I would say that there are aspects of God's character that David understood that I believe are particularly helpful to emphasise when leading worship.

David knew the grace of God, despite his own sinfulness

In Psalm 51 David acknowledges that not only does he commit sin, 'For I know my transgressions, and my sin is always before me' (verse 3), but also that his very nature is sinful, 'surely I have been a sinner from birth, sinful from the time my mother conceived me' (verse 5). Yet this did not result in condemnation, but in the recognition that, with repentance, God accepts him. 'The sacrifices of God are a broken spirit; a broken and contrite heart, O God, you will not despise' (verse 17). Putting it very simply, the gospel consists of three parts. First, the sinfulness of man that deserves the wrath of God; second, the atoning work of Christ; and third, the forgiveness of sin and our adoption as God's children. Many Christians know the first and second parts but do not come into the full joy and freedom of the last. It is essential that as worship leaders and musicians we really know, deep in our spirits, that 'there is now no condemnation for those who are in Christ Jesus' (Romans 8:1). While as individuals we must do all that we can to avoid sin, if we do fall, let us live in the truth that 'If we confess our sins, he is faithful and just and will forgive us our sins and purify us from all unrighteousness' (1 John 1:9).

Shortly after I became a Christian I visited a church where the emphasis of the meetings was clearly 'Thank you Lord – I know you have forgiven me.' This was evident in the joyfulness and gladness all around me. I have attended that church ever since! Grace liberates us! It is easy as worship leaders to focus on our unworthiness, and our sin. Yet to do this can bring heaviness. The joy of the gospel is that God says, 'Their sins and lawless acts I will remember no more' (Hebrews 10:17). If we devote ourselves to understanding the grace of God and emphasising it in our worship we will help to bring joy and gladness to our congregations.

There will be times as musicians and worship leaders when we need to claim this afresh for ourselves. Many of us have had the experience that, just prior to a meeting we are leading or playing at, we do something we regret. Perhaps we say an unkind word to someone or we dwell on an impure thought – whatever it is, it can lead us to fall into condemnation. Satan, who may have been encouraging us to do something only a moment ago, then turns into our accuser and reminds us of our unworthiness to lead others in worship. Of course, this is true – if we came to worship the Lord based on our own merits. But our lives are 'hidden with Christ in God' (Colossians 3:3). We can have 'confidence to enter the Most Holy Place' not by our own righteousness, but 'by the blood of Jesus' (Hebrews 10:19).

David knew that God had power to change him

Again, in Psalm 51, David prays 'Create in me a pure heart, O God and renew a steadfast spirit within me . . . Restore to me the joy of your salvation and grant me a willing spirit, to sustain me' (verses 10 and 12).

David knows that the Lord he serves is not just able to save him, but also to transform him. The gospel we sing about and the God we worship can change us. When we come to worship the Lord we are not just glorifying his name – we also make ourselves available to our Creator and Redeemer to work in our lives to change us. Romans 12 urges us 'in view of God's mercy' to offer your bodies as living sacrifices'. Amazed by God's love and grace towards us, we offer ourselves to him, to change us and mould us into the servants he wants us to be.

Sometimes at the end of worship times it is good to conclude with this concept and to lead the congregation in prayer in this way.

David knew that God was continually good

Psalm 23 is an anthem of God's goodness to his people, and reminds us that 'surely goodness and love will follow me all the days of my life' (verse 6). David experienced many days when it looked as if God's love was not following him at all, but it remained his declaration over his life. In Psalm 86:13, although he is being attacked by enemies he states, 'for great is your love towards me; you have delivered my soul from the depths of the grave.'

At any particular time there will be members of your congregation who are going through difficult times. It is invaluable to be reminded of the goodness of God, in spite of difficulty.

When we have experienced adversity but can see God's goodness to us, even in the midst of those difficulties, this produces character, hope and perseverance in us for the next time we face a difficult situation.

David had an eternal perspective

David knew that death was not the end – his relationship with the Lord would continue. We can see this clearly in Psalm 16, 'You will not abandon me to the grave . . . you will fill me with joy in your presence, with eternal pleasures at your right hand' and in Psalm 23, 'I will dwell in the house of the Lord for ever.'

It is important that we, too, have an eternal perspective in our worship. For most of us in the western world, where we have many material blessings, we can easily forget that this life is short compared with eternity. Yet anything the world can offer is trivial compared with the joys of heaven. It is good in our worship to focus upon the delights of the life to come.

Additionally, those in your congregation who are enduring times of trial and suffering can look forward to a time when there will be 'no more death or mourning or crying or pain' (Revelation 21:4).

I have also found it very helpful to meditate upon the passages in Revelation that give us a glimpse of the worship in heaven (for example Revelation chapters 4 and 5). These fill me with wonder and stir a longing in me for worship on the earth to be as it is in heaven. When so many people do not acknowledge Jesus as Lord it is helpful to remind ourselves that Jesus will return to judge the earth and to reign with his people forever.

'Who knows how to play the harp'

Saul's servant says that David knows how to play the harp. We could take this comment to be purely about musical gifting: after all, David was technically proficient in harp playing. However, I believe that the servant means more than this. There is clearly a spiritual dimension to Saul's torment. What was needed was not just a competent musician, but one who knew how to play the harp for that situation.

As church musicians our aim is not just to play but to play appropriately for a worship situation. I believe that David had learned how to play the harp effectively in worship, in a way in which he became a channel of God's blessing to those around him.

Many years ago I rarely played worship songs on my own at home. Then one day my wrists were injured in a car accident and I developed the symptoms of Repetitive Strain Injury or 'RSI' as it is more commonly known. For some weeks I could not play the guitar without experiencing pain and had to relinquish my musical role in our church for a while. Someone brought a prophetic word over me that, like the manager of a sports team, God had taken me away from the other players for special training. I was not pleased – I wanted to get back on the pitch! However, what happened was life changing. In time the injury improved: I couldn't play like before, but I could play a few simple chords on the guitar. I said to the Lord 'if that's all I can do to worship you, that's what I will do.' I began to devote time to worship, just playing a few chords and singing. My playing was transformed. It was less proficient technically – but I began to approach playing in a different way, within my limited capabilities, on the basis that all I would do was worship – no fancy riffs, just simple praise to the Lord. The RSI has improved (though it still gives me an occasional twinge) but my approach has remained the same.

Sometimes knowing 'how to play the harp' or any other instrument, is not a case of doing more grades or learning more chords (good though these are), but learning how best to play in worship. This is not something you can be told how to do – it has to come out of your relationship with the Lord.

Like the widow with her mite, God loves us to come with all we have and offer it to him, even if it is less than others possess. If we do not perceive ourselves as having a great deal of musical ability, but come to the Lord and submit the gifts we have, he can take them and use them for his glory, as he did with the five loaves and two fish.

David came to God in faith and expectation

In Psalm 40 David writes:

> I waited patiently for the Lord; he turned to me and
> heard my cry.
> He lifted me out of the slimy pit, out of the mud and
> mire;
> he set my feet on a rock and gave me a firm place to
> stand.
> He put a new song in my mouth, a hymn of praise to
> our God.

David saw his Lord not just as his Saviour but also as the provider of worship songs and music. It is not just that the Lord does wonderful things for us in lifting us from the pit of our sins, but his Spirit helps us to worship. If the Lord is the provider of our songs to him, then our expressions of praise and the music we play will never run dry because the Lord's creativity is inexhaustible. He is the God who makes all things new (Revelation 21:5), the one who causes the tree of life to yield fruit every month.

Every time we come to praise him we can expect his Spirit to inspire us, to make our worship fresh, to help us find new and creative expressions of worship.

Therefore, like David, we can approach worship times with faith and expectation, knowing that the Holy Spirit will inspire us and help us.

Conclusion

As we devote ourselves to spending time with the Lord we place ourselves in a position where he can work through us. Like David with Saul, our playing, singing and leading can then affect those around us as we minister God's grace and mercy to them.

Points to remember

- *David did not just provide some soothing music for Saul. God's grace and peace were communicated to Saul through David's playing.* As worship leaders and musicians, this is what we aim to do – to affect others through our playing and leading.

- *David had a special anointing but the Lord is also with us.*

- *David's anointing for worship was enhanced through his relationship with the Lord,* whom he sought after and to whom he communicated his feelings. David sought to abide in his presence, depend upon him, and enquire of him.

- *When David sang about the Lord it wasn't theoretical theology but real personal experience.* This is what impacts us when we read his psalms.

- *Our approach to playing instruments is to seek to be a channel of the Lord's blessing,* rather than just technically proficient, though this is also important.

- *God is not just our Saviour, but the One who continually provides inspiration in worship.*

Questions for personal application

1. Who would you say is particularly gifted in the area of worship (try to think of those whom you know personally as well as more widely-known figures)? Can you identify what contributes to their gifting, other than musical ability?

2. Think about the areas of longing for God, depending upon him and enquiring of him. In which of these areas do you believe your relationship with God is strong? Which are your weakest areas?

3. How would you describe your approach to playing your instrument/singing in worship? Is it different from playing at a secular concert? If so, in what ways?

4. Do you come to worship in expectation and faith that God will provide inspiration?

CHAPTER 3

Leading worship: Toppling giants
David and Goliath (1 Samuel 17)

The story of David and Goliath is an amazing passage of Scripture. We see the position of the Israelites, the people of God, completely transformed, from being 'dismayed and terrified' (1 Samuel 17:11) to routing their enemies. And this is all because they have been led by one person who has faith and trust in an almighty God, who vindicates those who look to him.

Worship can be a transforming experience for our congregations. When we come to worship we may be fearful about the situations that we face, yet once we have encountered a holy and omnipotent God in worship and reminded ourselves of his purposes and plans for us, we can feel victorious: we know that we are more than conquerors! Not because of anything we have done, but because of God's grace and our standing in Christ. What do I mean by victory? In this context I am referring to those situations in meetings where, as a congregation, you know that you have not just been singing some songs, but have experienced a measure of the presence* of

---

* Of course, God is always around us and the Psalmist notes in Psalm 139 that there is nowhere he can flee 'from [God's] presence' (verse 7). However, it is apparent from other Scriptures that there are occasions when people have a *particular* awareness of God's presence. We long for those occasions when we become acutely aware of his presence, and therefore his power, love and majesty. My prayer is that we have this kind of experience when we come to worship.

God and that he has led you into a greater understanding of his truth during the course of the worship time.

As worship leaders we can play a part in achieving this transformation, just as David did. However, when we come to lead our congregations we can feel as apprehensive as if we, too, are facing a giant!

Today's church needs champions like David who will actively seek to bring victory to the people. Champions who are not 'dismayed and terrified' of the challenge ahead of them, but who stride out boldly to take the challenge.

I believe that 1 Samuel 17 is not only a story about a military triumph but also gives us some clues as to how we, like David, can lead our people into a transforming experience.

David came as a servant (1 Samuel 17:17-19)

In his fight with Goliath David's intention was to serve the people, not to bring glory for himself.

As worship leaders, here are some ways we can serve the people:

- *Serving the people by praying that they will meet with God*

  Worship leading carries with it a responsibility to seek the Lord for the meeting and to intercede for the people we are leading. One of the best ways we can serve our congregations in worship is to pray that the Lord meets with them, speaks to them and guides them during worship. We can be tempted to intercede fervently about the meetings we are leading, and then be far less passionate about weeks when we are not directly involved. God is looking for worshippers – those who will seek him and intercede for his people regardless of whether they have a leadership role that week.

- *Serving the people by leading people from where they are*

  Sometimes the congregation is very ready to worship, at other times they need 'drawing' – gentle encouragement and some time to get themselves focused on the Lord. Leading a congregation can be like courting a woman. Come on too strong and you'll put her off! Instead she needs gentle and sensitive leading in the relationship! Sometimes you can feel as if you want to drive a congregation to worship when they aren't responding as enthusiastically as you would like, but it doesn't work to 'tell' people to praise God. We serve them by *inviting* them, not pressurising them.

It's worth taking a few moments to think about the mood of your congregation before you actually start the worship time. It isn't easy to detach yourself when you're feeling nervous and vulnerable! Ask the Holy Spirit to give you discernment and sensitivity to understand where people are at. I try to gauge how people are – is there a 'buzz' in the meeting room? If so, people are probably ready to worship. On the other hand, if it's, say, pouring with rain outside, people will probably need a few minutes to get their bearings and relax before they're ready to throw themselves into worship. It's worth also taking a few seconds in each song to think about how the congregation is doing, and what will serve them best in moving on to the next stage of meeting with the Lord. We are servants who want to engage the congregation in worship so that they encounter the Lord Jesus. We must never in any sense be 'performers' running through a 'set' of songs. If we come across in this way, whether consciously or unconsciously, we will encourage the congregation to be spectators rather than participators.

- ***Serving the people means selecting songs that your congregation respond to in worship***

  It is very tempting as a worship leader to choose songs that you like and that help you to worship. Some people see leading worship as an opportunity to indulge themselves in a Christian version of *Desert Island Discs*,* selecting their favourite songs. If you do this you will be serving yourself and not the people. Choose songs that help your congregation engage with God! There will be a diversity of taste in your congregation – some will only like songs by youthful worship artists, others think you should only sing songs of certain past eras as 'they don't write them like they used to'. However, you can tell when a song causes many in the congregation to respond in worship, rather than just a small grouping. I've always found it works best to include some of these songs, even if they're not all to my taste!

David brought his own style (1 Samuel 17:39-40)

Saul encouraged David to use traditional armour and weapons. It was important that David did not allow himself to be conformed to a traditional approach to fighting, but instead defeated Goliath by bringing his own style to the battle.

It is important that, as a worship leader, you bring your own style. When you were asked to lead worship you were chosen because of who you are. You do not need to imitate someone else. There may be many helpful lessons you can learn from observing others, but ultimately you must find your own way of leading.

David was in dialogue with leadership (1 Samuel 17:32-40)

In bringing our own style to worship leading, we must ensure that we are in communication with leadership. The whole tone of David's dealings with Saul is one of submission to him. I can't prove it, but based on how David acted in other

---

* *Desert Island Discs* is a radio programme in which celebrity guests are asked to imagine that they are marooned on a desert island but can only take eight pieces of music with them. The guest describes the significance of each piece to them personally, and the track is then played.

incidents in his life, I believe that if Saul had been insistent that David wore the armour, David would have done so.

Your church leadership will not be comfortable if you do something radically different in your church meetings without discussing it with them first. They take responsibility for the whole church. Their view of how well the idea will work and how your congregation will react to it will be broader and probably more balanced than yours. Over the years at our church I have been given more and more authority as a worship leader by the church leadership, probably more than less-experienced worship leaders. This has, however, been the product of relating with our leadership over many years and holding numerous discussions about worship. I would still, however, want to err on the side of checking with them if I wanted to do anything remotely different from the 'norm'. Please ensure that your church leadership are comfortable with what you want to do – you will spare yourself and your church from a lot of difficulties if you do!

If your church leadership aren't keen on your ideas to change things, it is tempting to sulk! A better way is to pour out your heart to God. As we leave the matter prayerfully with him, in the fullness of time he will bring changes, either to our own heart or to our leadership's.

David threw off other people's expectations (1 Samuel 17:39)

Saul's armour also reminds us that when we come to lead worship we can feel the burden of other people's expectations of how we should fight the battle. It is very easy to *feel* constrained as a worship leader through other people's expectations. You can feel under pressure to try to keep everyone happy, rather than doing what will really serve the people and please the Lord, which is to be led by the Holy Spirit. This can feel like heavy armour on you. At times like this I cast these burdens on God to be free to worship him myself.

David led when the people of God were despondent
(1 Samuel 17:11)

David was in a position of faith while 'Saul and all the Israelites were dismayed and terrified'. It can be difficult for you as a worship leader to remain positive when your church is going through a period when they are not seeing much in the way of victory, when people become despondent and apathetic.

The temptation is to 'wear the heavy armour'. When David put on Saul's armour he appears to have had difficulty even walking – if he had kept it on he would not have been able to take the battle to Goliath as he did (verse 48). The armour would have been purely defensive. We can fall into the trap of leading worship in what I would call a 'defensive' manner. Our expectations are low, and we are just seeking to get through the meeting without any faith that God will speak to his people or move among the congregation. We can end up just selecting songs that will keep the congregation mildly engaged, perhaps relying on techniques we have learned, but we have lost any sharpness to lead the people into the presence of the Lord.

David was not discouraged by the despondency within the Israelite camp, but clearly saw the battle as belonging to the Lord: 'The Lord . . . will deliver me from the hand of this Philistine' (verse 37). In these situations it is best to keep our eyes fixed 'on Jesus, the author and perfecter of our faith, who for the joy set before him endured the cross, scorning its shame, and sat down at the right hand of the throne of God. Consider him who endured such opposition from sinful men, so that you will not grow weary and lose heart' (Hebrews 12:2-3). Considering Jesus is the antidote against weariness and losing heart. As worship leaders, if we become discouraged we will not be able to lead our people effectively. Ephesians 6:10-18 reminds us of the spiritual battle that we are in and calls us to put on another kind of armour. The enemy is trying to discourage and defeat us. We need to remind ourselves of the truth of the gospel, that God has made us righteous through his Son, that we are saved by his grace. To do this requires a decision of the will, being proactive, like actively putting on armour. As I do this I then begin to change in my attitude – I realise that, through Christ, I can extinguish the flaming arrows of the evil one, and that through God's strength I can not only defend myself but also go onto the attack – I have the sword of the Spirit.

Ephesians chapter 6 then speaks of praying in the Spirit. I have often found it helpful to spend time seeking God in prayer, and particularly speaking in tongues, asking God for breakthrough. As I do this, my spirit is lifted and I begin to see the situation with faith.

I cannot pretend that leading congregations when they are feeling despondent is easy, particularly if that season lasts for some time, but it is important that we remain committed to the attack, not just to defence, in the battle we face.

David's public success was based on private victories
(1 Samuel 17:34-37)

David had won his private battles in defending his father's flock from both the lion and the bear. This equipped him to win the public battle against Goliath. We are unlikely to be able to lead the congregation well if we are privately in defeat in our personal battles, for example, against sin. The responsibility of leading worship should serve as an extra spur to us to lead holy lives.

David says to Saul: 'The Lord who delivered me from the paw of the lion and the paw of the bear will deliver me from the hand of this Philistine' (verse 37). David's relationship with God and his experience of his work in his life was very real. As we lead worship it should be based on a living relationship we have with the Lord. It is only from the reality of this that we can truly lead our congregations into a place of intimacy with our God.

This does not mean that we cannot lead worship when we are struggling with the circumstances of life, and various spiritual tests and trials. In fact, sometimes it is when things are at their most difficult and we feel that we are not coping particularly well that we are at our most dependent upon God and he uses us powerfully. In this manner the apostle Paul describes in 2 Corinthians 12:7-9 his struggles with his 'thorn in the flesh' and the Lord replies that 'My grace is sufficient for you, for my power is made perfect in weakness.'

David was prepared (1 Samuel 17:40)

David would never have succeeded in his battle if he hadn't prepared beforehand and obtained his ammunition! In worship leading, preparation is essential. It is an awesome responsibility to be asked to serve in leading people in their worship of the Lord.

David had to go to the stream to look for the weapons for his battle. As worship leaders, we need to spend time in God's presence preparing. His Holy Spirit is like an ever-flowing stream who will give us the direction and the insight we need to lead people. Remember – the Holy Spirit is the best worship leader there is and he is with you all the time: in your preparation and when you lead he is there to 'guide you into all truth' (John 16:13).

Some years ago, the Lord showed me a vision that revolutionised the way I prepare for worship leading. I saw a well and I drew water from it by cranking a handle at the side. When eventually the bucket came up I drank from it and the water was cool and wonderfully refreshing. Moreover, I saw that, supernaturally, other mouths were at the rim of the bucket too and, while I was drinking, they too were being refreshed.

I realised that God was saying that as I spent time in his presence not only would I be refreshed, but others too, as I shared what God had given me in my times alone with him. Since then, I have always prepared for leading worship by spending time worshipping the Lord on my own. Invariably he will remind me of a passage of Scripture or some aspect of his character that I then use as the theme of the worship time.

Sometimes the water has been easy to draw and I have felt that God has given me direction within about five minutes of my time alone with him. More frequently, I find it a struggle to 'draw up the bucket' and have sometimes wanted to give up! However, I find that if I am persistent then God honours my perseverance.

For more on preparation and other practicalities of worship leading please see Chapter 5 and Appendix I.

More ammunition than you need . . . (1 Samuel 17:40)

David found five stones. He only needed one. When we are preparing to lead worship we may find that God shows us many things – it's part of our reward as we earnestly seek him (Hebrews 11:6). It is tempting to feel that we need to bring all of these into the worship time, but usually this isn't effective. I often find that I get further down the track in my own preparation than what actually happens when we worship together as a church. I believe this is because at church meetings people are at different places in terms of their relationships with God – some have felt close to him that week, others have strayed from him – and so we can't all move forward rapidly together.

However, like a stone in a sling, what God gives you in your preparation will be powerful and effective.

Feeling vulnerable (1 Samuel 17:42)

I wonder how David felt when he came out to Goliath. It says that Goliath 'looked David over and saw he was only a boy, ruddy and handsome, and he despised him'. While you are unlikely to have people hurling abuse at you when you come to lead worship (!), you can hear voices of doubt in your head, perhaps playing upon any feeling you have of inadequacy or insecurity. For all the support of the army, for a moment David was on his own. It is like this when you come to lead worship – for all the support that you have from others there is a time when it is you who has to step out from the crowd and take a lead. You can feel very exposed and vulnerable.

David says 'You come against me with sword and spear and javelin, but I come against you in the name of the Lord Almighty' (verse 45). As worship leaders we do not represent ourselves, but we come in the name of the Lord, to bring due glory to his name. It is important that at these moments we do not focus on ourselves but begin to fix our eyes on Jesus (Hebrews 12:2). I try to consciously hand the worship time over to the Lord before, during and after the meeting, so that I don't get under pressure personally.

Speaking words of faith (1 Samuel 17:46)

David also speaks words of faith: 'this day the Lord will hand you over to me'. It is important that the words you speak to the congregation are words of faith. We shouldn't speak words of unreality – if we don't believe it, it's best not to say it! However, it is good to remind people about God's faithfulness, how he wants to meet with his people and how he wants to refresh them with his love. Quoting Scripture is very effective in declaring truth in your worship time, although I recommend that you keep it brief: long passages can cause the congregation's attention to wander!

David brought victory for all the people

We have largely focused on David in this chapter, but while he spearheaded the victory it was the whole army that seized hold of it. In verses 51 and 52 we read that 'When the Philistines saw that their hero was dead, they turned and ran.

Then the men of Israel and Judah surged forward with a shout and pursued the Philistines . . .'

Leading worship is not for our benefit – to build our reputations – it is to provide an environment in which our congregations can experience victory themselves. David arrived running an errand and ended up as the people's champion, but he was still serving. This must be the core of our attitude to leading, from beginning to end.

Why do we need breakthrough in worship?

Victory was important – not just because of the need to deal with the immediate threat of Goliath – it was deeper than that.

The Israelites had won many victories, but the Philistines were on Judah's land which God had promised to the people of Israel. In Judges 3:1-3, we see that the Philistines had never been removed from the land. The situation needed breakthrough to bring God's people into the complete victory of all that he had for them.

There is a parallel between this situation and worship. We have come a long way in church worship over the last thirty to forty years. Many battles have been won, and much ground taken in restoring worship to a more biblical pattern. Some of this 'ground' was:

- *Body ministry*

  Many years ago, most church services were characterised by 'one-man ministry' – i.e. meetings were led by one person. The pioneering generation of the 1960s to the early 1980s looked afresh at the New Testament, which clearly teaches that:

  > When you come together, everyone has a hymn, or a word of instruction, a revelation, a tongue or an interpretation. All of these must be done for the strengthening of the church. *1 Corinthians 14:26*

Many churches went through radical changes in order to incorporate 'body ministry' into church life, so that there was an environment in which members of the congregation could contribute.

- *Gifts of the Spirit*

  As a growing number of individuals received the baptism in the Holy Spirit there was an increasing awareness that the gifts of the Spirit (1 Corinthians 12:7-11) had not ceased. Some pioneered their restoration in church worship.

- *A sense of the spontaneous*

  As you read through the book of Acts, particularly Acts 2:1-4, 42-47, there appears to be excitement whenever the church gathers together. They did not know what would happen next! The Holy Spirit was doing amazing things among them, and they responded to his leading. Similarly, there was a genuine sense when the church gathered to worship in this 'reforming' period that no one knew which direction each worship time would go in. There was excitement about worshipping together. Many mistakes and 'wrong turnings' were made but there was a great sense of spontaneity at church gatherings.

- *Greater cultural relevance*

  While this is not explicitly a biblical issue, church services were becoming less culturally relevant in style and format. Hymns were largely based on musical styles from the nineteenth century, which seemed at odds with a generation raised on pop and rock music. Worship music was updated to reflect this and church meetings became more informal, just as society had lost much of its formality. This made it easier for those who had no experience of church life to adapt to it, rather than feeling they had entered a cultural time warp every time they went through the doors of a church building!

It's sometimes hard to appreciate just how difficult a process this was. Sadly, there were disagreements, sometimes splits, as some church members were gripped with passionate reforming zeal and challenged traditions that other church members wished to retain. It truly was a battle and there was great cost as such changes were implemented. To receive the 'new wine', the 'wineskin' had to be replaced.

Now, in a new millennium, with so much ground already taken are we are in danger of being complacent? Do we feel that there are no more battles to be won and we can just 'settle' in the 'land' we have already gained?

The reality is that for us, just like the Israelite army, there is still a lot of ground to be taken. Furthermore, I wonder if we have lost some of the pioneering spirit of the 1960s to early 1980s, and actually lost some ground.

We believed 'one-man ministry' was unbiblical – but have we found that, in practice, instead of 'body ministry', many worship times are led by a worship leader with very little contribution from anyone else? Have we exchanged one form of one-man ministry for another?

Having pressed through much change (some of it involving considerable pain) in order to see spiritual gifts restored to our churches, are we now finding that we can go through meetings without witnessing the gifts of the Spirit?

Have we also lost some of our passion to see true New Testament worship in our churches? Are we still trying to take ground or have we settled?

Do you arrive at your church meeting with a genuine sense of expectation, not knowing what will happen, but certain that you will encounter the presence of God and that you will leave the meeting encouraged and challenged? Or do you feel that the worship time will consist of singing a few songs with little sense of God's presence?

To continue our battle analogy, what is 'victory' in worship? Perhaps in summary it is biblically-based worship that glorifies

God in spirit and in truth and has the powerful dynamic of being led by the Holy Spirit. Let's consider in more detail what the 'ground' is that needs to be taken.

Another look at Scripture – what worship should be like

1. An awesome sense of the presence of God

Many churches regularly experience a sense of the presence of God during worship times, and we thank the Lord with all our hearts for this. But when we measure this against some of the episodes in Scripture we find that there is so much more! I long for times like Isaiah 6 where Isaiah is completely overwhelmed with the presence of the Lord. Similarly, the apostle John, in the opening chapter of Revelation, is surprised by an unexpected, awe-inspiring encounter with the risen Lord Jesus. If we truly believe that the Lord wants to meet with his people in worship, then these are the sort of meetings with the Lord that we must pray and seek God for.

2. Expecting the unexpected: God setting his agenda

In 2 Chronicles 5:13-14 we read how the presence of God is so overwhelming at the opening of Solomon's temple, in the form of a cloud of God's glory, that the priests could not perform their service. It was as if God was setting the agenda for the meeting rather than man. Similarly, in Acts 2, at a meeting of the early church, the Holy Spirit visits the disciples in a dramatic way and leads them in an evangelistic breakthrough.

I long for meetings such as this, where there is an overwhelming sense of God leading his people. In the mid-1990s many churches in the UK and elsewhere experienced an outpouring of the Holy Spirit. One of the most exciting things was, as one person put it, that God was 'inviting us to one of his meetings', rather than him attending ours! There was a sense of spontaneity, of excitement, of being on an adventure together, which I would love to recapture.

3. An outpouring of the gifts of the Spirit
(1 Corinthians 12:7-11)

Now to each one the manifestation of the Spirit is given for the common good.

- To one there is given through the Spirit the **message of wisdom**,
- to another the **message of knowledge** by means of the same Spirit,
- to another **faith** by the same Spirit,
- to another **gifts of healing** by that one Spirit,
- to another **miraculous powers**,
- to another **prophecy**,
- to another **the ability to distinguish between spirits**,
- to another **the ability to speak in different kinds of tongues**,
- and to still another the **interpretation of tongues**.

(bold type is my emphasis)

It seems that when the New Testament church gathered together spiritual gifts were a regular occurrence. Are we experiencing a full expression of spiritual gifts in today's worship meetings? If not, it's ground still to be taken.

Furthermore, the range of spiritual gifts at our meetings can be limited. At our church we regularly experience tongues and interpretations, prophecy and messages of knowledge. We are very thankful for this. However, we have yet to witness more than the occasional healing and I do not believe that we have ever seen 'miraculous powers'. I believe that Paul's writings indicate that each of these gifts were regularly experienced in the early church and we long for all of them to be restored to us.

4. Anointed prophecy

I believe that the Lord has a greater dimension of prophecy for his church. In Acts 13:2 it says:

> While they (the apostles) were worshipping the Lord
> and fasting, the Holy Spirit said, 'Set apart for me Barnabas
> and Saul for the work to which I have called them.'

This was more than just a word of encouragement for the church (much as we need and appreciate such words) – it was revelation of a major strategic move for the church that impacted the known world. It is interesting to note that in the passages from Isaiah 6 and Revelation 1 mentioned above an overwhelming sense of God's presence is followed by powerful prophetic words. While it is unrealistic to expect prophecies of such significance at every church meeting, I believe that there is a greater anointing in the prophetic for us to experience.

5. A wealth of participation

> When you come together, everyone has a hymn, or a
> word of instruction, a revelation, a tongue or an inter-
> pretation.   *1 Corinthians 14:26*

New Testament church meetings appear to have many members of the congregation participating. Some of these were undoubtedly spiritual gifts, but there would be other forms of participation. 'Hymns' of praise – perhaps spontaneous songs by someone in the congregation, or someone other than the worship leader starting to sing an appropriate worship song that the congregation knows and joins in with. It is also encouraging when members of the congregation pray prayers of thanksgiving to God. Some of these bring to mind 'instruction' and 'revelation' as they are inspired and full of truth about who God is and what he has done.

Worship times were not 'one-man ministry' in the early church. If we truly believe in 'body ministry', with each member playing a part, then our church meetings will reflect this, with involvement from many members of the body.

6. Unbelievers convicted

At New Testament worship times unbelievers were convicted of sin by the presence of the Lord.

> But if an unbeliever or someone who does not understand comes in while everybody is prophesying, he will be convinced by all that he is a sinner and will be judged by all, and the secrets of his heart will be laid bare. So he will fall down and worship God, exclaiming, 'God is really among you!' *1 Corinthians 14:24-25*

There is a clear link between salvation and spiritual gifts. One man came to our church and heard three words of knowledge given in the meeting that were so accurate about him that he realised that God knew all about him. He became a Christian that day.

In Acts 2 a church meeting becomes an 'open air', leading to three thousand being saved. While this incorporated an obviously anointed gospel message, once again there is a link between the presence of God in the church gathering and salvation of unbelievers.

I once heard a story relating to a church in another part of the world that is experiencing revival. Twenty-five soldiers attended a meeting at which there was a powerful sense of the Lord's presence. Twenty-four of them ran to the front to become Christians – the other one fled from the church. How wonderful to be in a meeting where unbelievers are faced with a clear choice – *to run to* God or *run away from* him, rather than being able to *walk away* commenting that 'the singing was lovely!'

7. Victory over the enemy

In 2 Chronicles 20:21-26 we see how praise and worship defeats a physical enemy. I believe that in the New Testament age, praise is a powerful weapon against the spiritual forces that oppose the Lord's work. 1 Samuel 16:23 gives a further example of the change in the spiritual atmosphere that can result from an anointed musician worshipping the Lord with his or her instrument.

I cannot tell you how this happens, but what Scripture makes clear is that musicians playing in worship to God and singers expressing truth about God have a powerful impact on situations. As we grasp this it will cause us to play and sing in faith that we really do make a difference.

8. Extravagant, expressive praise and worship

When the ark is restored to Jerusalem in 2 Samuel 6:14 David worships by dancing before the Lord *with all his might.*

The psalms, too, are full of extravagant praise, physically expressed. Psalm 95:1-6 says:

> Come, let us sing for joy to the Lord;
> let us *shout aloud* to the Rock of our salvation . . .
> Come, let us *bow down* in worship,
> let us *kneel* before the Lord our Maker

Psalm 149:3 says, 'Let them [Israel] praise his name with dancing.'

Biblical worship involves the participants 100 per cent: body, mind and spirit. Yet often when we praise God we are not engaged to this degree!

Facing giants

To bring change, to take the ground that still needs to be taken, requires great courage and passion. As we have seen, Saul's army was hardly gripped with zeal!

It's easy for us to be critical, but, to be fair, they were facing a giant! Scripture gives a detailed description of his physique and armoury to leave us in no doubt that Goliath was an intimidating figure.

If we are to take ground we must remember that we are facing some 'giants' of our own, and that these may cause us to feel just like Saul and his army!

- *The giant of apathy*

  If taking ground involves courage, determination, passion and effort, then we may find ourselves saying that it isn't worth bothering – things are fine as they are!

- *The giant of tradition*

  Even among churches which have made great efforts to remove tradition in worship we can easily find that our meetings follow predictable patterns and styles. Doing even slightly different things can unsettle the congregation and provoke opposition from some members. It is easy to slip into a mindset of associating tradition with old styles of music. In fact, any reliance on forms of worship, as opposed to having a heart that seeks after the presence of God and relies upon the Holy Spirit for the meeting, is serving the giant of tradition rather than reflecting biblical worship.

- *The giant of uncertainty*

  If we are truly taking ground we will be entering territory that we are unfamiliar with.

- *The giant of fear of failure*

  Whoever fought Goliath would have to face the fact that losing meant certain death, and could also bring a sense of humiliation to his family – 'These are the relatives of the guy that lost us the battle.' Fear of failure can be paralysing. Fortunately we are not in David's position; he had only one chance to succeed or fail. We admire and relate to biblical figures, such as Peter, who had a succession of situations where he boldly tried to do something, only to fail. We recognise that he learned from these failures and eventually emerged as the 'rock' Jesus called him to be. While we admire Peter for his courage, we ourselves can be reluctant to take risks.

Conclusion

While we have won many battles in the area of worship, there's still a lot of ground to be taken. A giant is on the land – land the church is called to occupy in worship.

Can we take the land? Of course we can. David said 'The Lord who delivered me from the paw of the lion and the paw of the bear will deliver me from the hand of this Philistine' (1 Samuel 17:37). The God who has helped us win the battles of the past will help us to take ground in the future. Ultimately, despite facing giants, it's an unequal contest! David says, 'Who is this uncircumcised Philistine that he should defy the armies of the living God' (verse 26). Like Elisha's servant, we need to grasp that although we have opposition, 'Those who are with us are more than those who are with them' (2 Kings 6:16).

Today's church needs champions like David who will actively seek to take the ground. People who are not 'dismayed and terrified', but who boldly stride out to take the challenge.

Points to remember

- *The Israelites were transformed.* Worship can be a transforming experience for our churches.

- *David came to the battle as a servant.* As worship leaders and musicians our role is to serve the church.

- *Like David we need to bring our own style,* but make sure we discuss any proposed changes with our church leadership well in advance of the meeting!

- *It was vital that David was prepared.* It is an essential part of worship leading too!

- *David may have felt vulnerable in leading,* but God was with him.

- *As churches in the UK, we have seen worship make great progress in the last 30 to 40 years,* but there is so much more to come. We must be ready to take on some giants to bring the church into victory.

Questions for personal application

1. In which areas of biblical worship is your church strong? What areas would you like to see it develop in?

2. Think back over particularly memorable times of worship you have experienced. What were the features that made these times special?

3. How do you believe that the full spectrum of biblical worship will be restored to the church? What part can you play in this?

CHAPTER 4

Implementing a vision
(2 Samuel 6; 1 Chronicles 13, 15)

Let us move forward two decades. David has become king. So much has been achieved, and David, after many trials and struggles, is now on the throne, in accordance with the anointing he received from Samuel all those years ago.

It would have been tempting to settle in the position God had placed him in. He could have felt justified in enjoying a period of rest and consolidation after the turbulence of the past years. But David knew that something was lacking. God had more for his people. David became gripped by a vision. He wished to see the ark of the covenant that signified the presence of God, restored to be, once again, among the people of God.

After all the battles David had fought and won, after all the difficulties he had encountered and overcome in the past, surely this would be an easy task. Yet the road to restoration was costly, causing David to wonder whether he would ever be able to achieve the godly objective he desired. When he eventually attained it he received sharp criticism from an unexpected source that must have hurt him deeply.

As musicians and worship leaders, we will each have our own dreams and visions. Perhaps it is to experience a fresh sense of the presence of God restored to your church. Perhaps it is to have the gifts of the Spirit more regularly in your church meetings. Maybe it is to establish a group of musicians into a band that works together to bring inspiring worship to your church. The reward of achieving your objective will be tremendously satisfying, but we must be mindful that the route we are taking is not an easy one. We can learn from David that difficulties we encounter may be part of the process we have to go through. Sometimes God wants us to persevere in order to prove that our desire is permanent, not transient.

Before we look at David's actions, we need to understand the significance of the ark. The ark symbolised the presence of God among his people. It is first referred to in Exodus 25, when God directs the people of Israel to construct it, giving very detailed instructions. In Numbers 10:33-36 there is the clear link between the cloud of the presence of God and the ark. The ark had been present in the book of Joshua when the Israelites had crossed the River Jordan (chapter 3), and in taking the city of Jericho (chapter 6). When it was captured by the Philistines in 1 Samuel 4 its loss was so keenly felt that Eli, high priest in Israel, collapsed and died. J. A. Thompson* sees the significance of the ark not as an object in itself, but in what it represents: the mobile presence of God and his uncompromising holiness among his people.

David's desire was a godly one

Restoring the ark to the people of Israel would be a major step forward for the nation, to restore some of the spiritual heritage of the people. We read in 1 Chronicles 13:3 that Israel did not enquire of the ark of God during Saul's reign. Now David had an opportunity to reinstate what had been lost.

When we face difficulties and opposition it is tempting to listen to doubts that our vision is not from God, after all.

---

* J. A. Thompson, *1 & 2 Chronicles (New American Commentary)*, Nashville, Broadman & Holman, 1994.

David went through many struggles to achieve his vision, yet his desire was right and godly. With the benefit of hindsight we can clearly see that David's vision was right. Equally we can see that his first attempt at implementing it was wrong!

Sometimes our attempts to implement a vision fail, not because the idea is wrong but because there are other flaws. It may be our methods; it may be our timing. We may be working with the wrong team of people or in the wrong situation. Perhaps our vision will be fulfilled later.

To use an example from another biblical figure, Joseph, the original visions he had were clearly from God. Yet it would take many years, and many trials, for those dreams to become reality, as we can see from Genesis chapters 37 to 50.

David's idea had the support of the people

While David was king, and therefore could give orders without reference to others, he does not act unilaterally. In 1 Chronicles 13 he consults 'the whole assembly of Israel' (verse 2), who 'agreed to do this (i.e. bring back the ark) because it seemed right to all the people'.

It is always good to consult others before trying to implement our visions. Our ideas are refined and adapted through the wisdom of others and we are strengthened if others express support.

David did not enquire of the Lord

As we read through the scriptural accounts of David's life it is notable how often he seeks the Lord before making major decisions. For example, in 2 Samuel 5, before fighting the Philistines, he enquires of the Lord not once, but twice, and receives detailed battle tactics!

It therefore seems strange that David does not appear to seek the Lord before bringing back the ark. Perhaps David was being casual – he assumed that the Lord would bless whatever he did. Or perhaps he was proud: after all he had achieved, maybe this was something he could accomplish in his own strength.

It is essential to commit our ideas prayerfully to the Lord. It is easy to ask God's blessing on a project, but not really be open to hearing his counsel, which may direct us to change our idea, or delay it. Sometimes we can end up committing ourselves and others to a project without consulting the Lord – and then demand his blessing upon it! It is important to know a sense of the Lord's approval of our vision *before* trying to implement it. Sometimes this can occur through God speaking directly to us. At other times it may be through circumstances or things other people say. My experience is that, however the guidance is received, I *know* when God is directing me. We must, however, be open to the fact that our ideas can sometimes become so important to us that we can cease to be objective about them. If we discuss our proposals with mature Christians they can provide us with a 'reality check'. Doing so can make us feel vulnerable, and we need grace to receive their constructive criticism if they do not respond with wholehearted enthusiasm.

If our vision is the Lord's will he will give us clarity over the timing and the means to achieve what we have in mind. It is remarkable how often 'coincidences' occur when we seek God's guidance. We may find opportunities opening up for precisely what we desired. Other people, unprompted, may share with us the fact that they have the same vision. Equally we may find that God makes it clear to us that now is not the right time for us to try to implement our vision.

David follows the ways of unbelievers

In 1 Samuel 6 we read that the Philistines returned the ark to Israel by putting it on a cart. David appears to follow their example rather than examining Scriptures such as Exodus

25:12-14 and Numbers 4:5-6, 15, which give detailed clarification about the ark and how it is to be transported. The latter passage clearly points to the fact that only the priests should carry it, and also contains a strong warning: 'the Kohathites are to come to do the carrying. But they must not touch the holy things or they will die.'

We have at all times to remember that our standards should always be taken from Scripture, not from the world. The world has particular ways of achieving its ends, often by ruthlessly and selfishly pursing a goal with little respect for others. We are called to live not by the ways of the world, but with Scripture as our standard.

Uzzah was familiar with the ark

In 1 Samuel 7 we read that the ark was held by a man named Abinadab. In 2 Samuel 6 we find out that Uzzah was Abinadab's son. He had grown up with the ark in his household for over twenty years. He would have been familiar with it. Was he over-familiar with it, and did he not appreciate its power and significance?

We may have been Christians a long time; perhaps we have even grown up in a family committed to a church. We can sometimes be in danger of taking God's approval for granted. It is important that we recognise with whom we are dealing. The mistake the Israelites made when they lost the ark to the Philistines was to believe that the presence of the ark *guaranteed* them success rather than appreciating that the ark symbolised the presence of a person, a person who can never be manipulated by men and women who want him to do their will.

If we ever display a careless, over-familiar attitude to God and to his presence we may be in for a shock! While the Lord promises to be there when even 'two or three come together in my name' (Matthew 18:20) this does not mean that there is a supernatural law that God is always powerfully present when three Christians are together, and that he automatically endorses every Christian meeting. Instead, in my view, the verse presupposes that those individuals are gathering with a rightful, humble attitude, seeking the presence of the Lord.

David was angry when his initial plan failed (2 Samuel 6:8)

When Uzzah was struck down, David was angry. The Bible does not say who he was angry with. There are a few possibilities:

- *Uzzah* – surely someone so used to the ark should have known not to touch it?

- *Himself* – David may have been angry with himself. This may have been for not enquiring of the Lord, for not researching Scripture, for starting a project that had led to Uzzah's death, or for causing disappointment to the people of God.

- *Other people* – why didn't one of the Levites speak up about the instructions of Scripture?

- *God* – David may have even been angry with the Lord for not blessing his plan, or at least not preventing the tragedy when David believed he was doing the right thing!

When our plans to implement our visions fail we can become angry. We experience a sense of loss, and resentment may well be a consequence. Like David, we may be angry with:

- *Ourselves*

- *Other people* whom we may feel have let us down, got in our way, or (in our opinion) not been sufficiently supportive

- *The Lord himself* – why did he not give us success as we believed we were carrying out his will?

These are natural feelings, but it is important that we deal with them in the right way. David's approach, as seen by the psalms, is not to criticise others, or to keep his feelings inside him, but instead to pour out his heart to God.

- In Psalm 22 David asks, 'My God, my God, why have you forsaken me?'
- In Psalm 6 he says to God 'my soul is in anguish'.

When we are disappointed we can become bitter towards God and/or others. Expressing our feelings to the Lord leads to resolution – Psalm 4 ends with 'I will lie down and sleep in peace, for you alone, O Lord, make me dwell in safety'. Psalm 6 ends with 'The Lord has heard my cry for mercy; the Lord accepts my prayer.' God is big enough to take our anger and our anguish and to lead us to resolution and to fresh hope. If we express our anguish to God, yet are in submission to his will, we will find, over time, that our feelings are resolved.

It is healthy to ventilate our feelings 'vertically' – by pouring out our hearts to God. Problems arise when we ventilate 'horizontally' – and other people experience our anger. This can damage our relationships. Once we have achieved a sense of resolution with God, it is easier to express our disappointment to others in a constructive, gracious way.

David is tempted to relinquish his vision (2 Samuel 6:9)

After Uzzah's death David said, ' "How can the ark of the Lord ever come to me?" He was not willing to take the ark of the Lord to be with him in the City of David. Instead, he took it aside to the house of Obed-Edom the Gittite.'

The painful disappointment and tragedy leads him to question whether he will ever be able to achieve his dream. After feeling angry he was tempted to give up! This may well be our experience, too.

Rather than take the ark to Jerusalem, it ends up in the house of Obed-Edom. David had brought the ark some distance, but is now tempted to settle for less than his original goal. Disappointment can lead us to compromise our visions.

David's failure is public

When we are not in leadership our mistakes tend only to affect ourselves and a few others. The greater our leadership role, the more people we affect when we mess things up! David had to face the fact that this incident was not just a personal failure but would have been talked about throughout the nation. All of Israel would have been disappointed, and David may well have been the target of criticism.

We can be eager to have the profile and influence of a leadership position, but here is another part of the leadership package! Public failure is even more painful than private errors!

David submits himself to the will of God

Andrew Hill in his commentary on 1 and 2 Chronicles* sees the abandonment of the ark at the house of Obed-Edom as an indication of David's submission to God's will. This is consistent with David's expression of submission in Psalm 40:

> Sacrifice and offering you did not desire, but my ears
>   you have pierced;
> burnt offerings and sin offerings you did not require.
> Then I said, 'Here I am, I have come – it is written
>   about me in the scroll.
> I desire to do you will, O my God;
> your law is within my heart.'   *Psalm 40:6-8*

We should therefore read David's reaction not as one of petulance or despair, but of submitting himself to God, trusting that the Lord will make his way known to David for the future. This is the attitude that will lead us to fulfilment as God does not despise 'a broken and contrite heart' (Psalm 51:17) but uses individuals who come before him in this way.

---

* Andrew Hill, *1 & 2 Chronicles (The NIV Application Commentary)*, Zondervan, 2003.

David is reminded of the importance of his vision
(2 Samuel 6:12)

David is angry and tempted to give up, but ultimately God will not let David abandon the vision.

David is told that the ark has brought blessing to Obed-Edom's household and David understands that this blessing is not just for one family but for the whole nation to enjoy. God may cause us to experience, either on a small scale or in a different setting, the blessing that he wants us to bring to the people we serve.

If our visions and dreams are from the Lord, he will find ways to remind us of what he has put in our hearts. He will fan back into flame the dying embers of ideas he has given us.

David enquired of the Lord

We have already seen that David's first attempt ended in failure because he did not enquire of the Lord or follow God's instructions for moving the ark. For David's second attempt there is no explicit reference to David enquiring of the Lord, or to him searching the Scriptures for guidance; however, his clear direction, his reference to the role of the Levites in 1 Chronicles 15:2, and his ultimate success, are clear indications that he sought the Lord.

Success came from planning, and involving a 'team'

The two accounts in Chronicles of the ark's transportation are in marked contrast to each other in the extent to which others are involved and the level of detail regarding the organisation of the event. While in 1 Chronicles 13 David assembled all the Israelites (verse 5) there is no indication of the role others were to play. In 1 Chronicles 15 there is clearly an attention to detail, with many people given specific tasks.

Not only does the involvement of a team reduce the workload for the leader, but it allows others to fully participate in the vision. Their gifts and experience blend with ours and bring a greater depth to our original plans.

Involving others requires greater planning on our part. We can see that David was meticulous in his organisation. This was certainly an ingredient in his success.

David had an attitude of humility

There is no evidence that David was proud during his first attempt to transport the ark. However, he is clearly humble second time around:

- *David is wearing a linen ephod*

  This was a priestly garment worn by those who served before the Lord in his sanctuary. David is careful not to be seen as a conquering king, but as a priestly servant. His garment was distinct from the special ephod worn by the high priest – David is not exalting himself to an office he was not called to. His attitude is one of humility and submission to the will of God.

- *David brings sacrifices*

  Again, this is an indication of David's attitude of submission and humility before the Lord.

David brought success for the people

We could see the restoration of the ark as a personal triumph for David. I am sure that he would have preferred to view it as a success for all God's people. It is tempting to see ministry success in a personal way, either for ourselves or for others who have led such ventures. It is preferable to see it as a triumph for the community of believers.

David experienced opposition (2 Samuel 6:20-23)

Even after an occasion that was full of celebration, David still experiences opposition. The criticism is shocking for the reader. We do not know whether it was unexpected for David, but Michal's tone is in marked contrast to the celebratory mood in the city. As leaders we may find ourselves the subject of criticism even when there has been a major breakthrough in our church life. Such opposition reminds us that our struggle is not against flesh and blood – we have an enemy who would seek to damage us, whether things are going well or badly! As well as reminding us that spiritual opposition is unrelenting, the criticism would have helped to keep David in a state of humility and not focussing on his personal success.

Criticism can be helpful in identifying areas for improvement. However, Michal's words are unconstructive and ungracious. When someone despises, rather than brings constructive criticism, their words usually have no merit and we should pay little heed to them.

David learns through the experience

When we are experiencing difficulties in implementing our visions, it is tempting to wish that everything was easy. However, if we have to persevere in order to achieve the task God has given us it helps us to become more mature in our faith.

D. F. Payne in his commentary on 2 Samuel picks out two lessons learned – by David and by the people of Israel:

> David learned that he was not free to do as he liked with the ark; still less could he manipulate the God represented by the ark.
>
> Their God Yahweh was more powerful than any foreign attackers or oppressors. It also taught them that respect for God's holiness was essential to the well-being of the community.*

As we persevere through difficulties and finally see our vision implemented we know that it is not just external situations

---

* D. F. Payne, *New Bible Commentary*, IVP, 1994.

that have changed: we have been transformed into more mature Christians through the process.

If you are involved in worship I would encourage you to hold onto the vision God has given you. If it has been given to you by God he will bring it to completion, perhaps through many trials and setbacks, but, like David, to ultimate success.

Points to remember

- *David's desire was a godly one,* even though it did not succeed the first time.
- *David's idea had the support of the people.* It is good to consult others.
- *David did not enquire of the Lord the first time round –* and look what happened!
- *If we ever get over-familiar in our attitude to God, we may be in for a shock!*
- *If our initial plan fails we may, like David, get angry.* It is important that we express our feelings to God.
- *We may be tempted to relinquish God's vision after our disappointments,* but he may remind us of the importance of the vision
- *We are more likely to be successful if we plan thoroughly and involve a team.*
- *Even when what you do is of God, you can still get opposition from some people!*

Questions for personal application

1. Have you experienced disappointment in trying to fulfil a vision? What lessons have you learned from the experience?
2. What godly ambitions have remained with you for a period of years?

3. Have you observed others seeking to fulfil their visions? What have you learned about the process?

4. Have you shared your vision with others who can provide mature and constructive advice?

CHAPTER 5

Leading people in worship
(1 Chronicles 15, 16)

In 1 Chronicles 15 and 16 we see David leading the people of God in worship as he restores the ark of the covenant, which symbolised and signified the presence of God, to Jerusalem (the city of God). He had the joy of leading the people of God in worship. Yet with this privilege comes responsibility.

It is an honour for us to lead members of our congregations in worship whether the setting is large or small. But with these opportunities comes the need to ensure that we are faithful and diligent in what we have been given to do.

Being spiritually prepared

We saw in the previous chapter that David's first attempt to restore the ark in 2 Samuel 6 ended in failure because he did not enquire of the Lord or follow God's instructions for moving the ark.

For David's second attempt there is no explicit reference in 1 Chronicles 15 to David enquiring of the Lord, or to him searching the Scriptures for guidance. Instead, we see the evidence of it in the clarity of his leading and his ultimate success. Verses 12 to 16 show the clear direction and leadership he brings to God's people.

Why does Scripture not tell us explicitly of his communication with God? I believe that this is because it was part of David's private preparation, his secret relationship with the Lord.

Jesus teaches us of the importance of the secret relationship with God in Matthew 6:6:

> When you pray, go into your room, close the door and pray to your Father, who is unseen. Then your Father, who sees what is done in secret, will reward you.

As we come to lead worship it is vital that we spend time with the Lord asking him for anointing and direction. Others will not see the effort you put into preparing: that is part of your private relationship with the Lord. They will see the results. The way that you lead will be born out of your relationship with the Lord. The direction you give to the meeting will come from your time with him on your own. Our church leaders have entrusted us with a great responsibility in asking us to lead worship. It is vital to ensure we are adequately prepared spiritually.

David had clear direction as to how he would restore the ark. My own aim in preparing to lead worship is to find a theme – God's direction for the meeting. In Chapter 3 I wrote about 'drawing water from the well' (see Isaiah 12:3). I do this by setting aside time to worship the Lord and to seek him for the meeting I will be leading. As I do this I find myself drawn to a particular aspect of God's character, or to something that he has done, usually expressed by a particular passage of Scripture. I know when I have my theme because, in my personal worship time, what may be a very familiar doctrine or verse of Scripture suddenly feels fresh and alive, infused with power.

An example of a verse that has come across to me in this way is Psalm 103:13: 'As a father has compassion on his children, so the Lord has compassion on those who fear him.' I will then prepare my song list around the theme of God's fatherly love for us. Sometimes this 'theme' comes to me very quickly; at other times it does feel like 'drawing water from a well': it is hard work and takes ages for anything to come up! I am tempted to give up but I find that, as I persevere, God speaks to me.

Song lists

If there is little thematic coherence between songs there is unlikely to be a sense of flow; the congregation is being asked to focus on different aspects of God's character as the subject of each song changes!

To avoid this it is good to select songs that fit the theme that God has given you. After my initial preparation I prepare a list of every song I know that might possibly suit the direction I believe God has given me. This is often very long! Later I will review the list and reduce it to the most suitable songs.

The number of songs we ultimately need depends, of course, on the length of the meeting. Our Sunday morning meetings have approximately forty-five minutes of worship. As we allow space for members of the congregation to bring spiritual gifts and other contributions, we would normally sing no more than five or six songs in this time. My list is therefore about ten songs, giving me plenty of flexibility to modify the choice of songs we sing based on the direction the worship time is taking. Sometimes, however, we will sing a song outside of the list altogether, if, during the course of the meeting, it feels appropriate to do so.

After composing my list I will then put the songs into a rough order. Psalm 95 gives us a model for worship times:

> Come, let us sing for joy to the Lord;
> let us shout aloud to the Rock of our salvation.
> Let us come before him with thanksgiving
> and extol him with music and song . . .   *Psalm 95:1-2*

This first block of verses implies exuberance with joyful singing, shouting and extolling (to 'praise highly'*). The next few verses of the psalm speak of more reverent reflection: bowing, kneeling and a sense of adoration.

---

* *Chambers Twentieth Century Dictionary*, W. & R. Chambers Ltd, 1972. ISBN 0 550 10206X.

> Come, let us bow down in worship,
> let us kneel before the Lord our Maker. *Psalm 95:6-7*

This psalm is a template for most worship times – songs for joyful singing at the beginning, moving on to more reverent, reflective songs.

I have personally found that this pattern works for most worship meetings. I have occasionally started meetings with slow songs and then moved on to more joyful songs later. My experience is that this only works when I am completely confident that this is how the Holy Spirit wants me to lead. Otherwise it tends not to work! Ninety-five per cent of the time I lead according to the pattern of Psalm 95.

Song categories

It can be helpful to divide the song lists into categories that fit the model of Psalm 95.

- *Joyful* – up-tempo songs to help the congregation focus on the Lord, e.g. 'Give thanks to the Lord, our God and King' by Chris Tomlin, or 'Beautiful One' by Tim Hughes.

- *Bridge song* – I will often use a song that is a bit slower than the first songs, that provides a link between the joyful and more reflective phases of worship. An example of this would be 'O Jesus Son of God (Light of the World)' by Matt Redman.

- *Worship songs* – fitting in with the second phase of Psalm 95. I tend to divide these into two sub-categories – those that have a firmer tempo, like 'Worthy, you are worthy' by Matt Redman, and those that are more intimate, such as 'I will offer up my life', again by Matt Redman or 'We bow down' by Viola Grafstrom.

You may find it helpful to go through songbooks and categorise them into types of songs, and possibly into themes. Some songbooks have a thematic index, which you may find helpful.

Leaving room for the spontaneous

There is a further phase within Psalm 95:

> Today, if you hear his voice do not harden your hearts . . .
>
> *Psalm 95:7-8*

This is clearly a prophetic word being given in the midst of worship. It is important to leave room for the spontaneous – for example, for a prophetic contribution to be brought and for the direction of the worship time to change, if appropriate. It is best not to try to prepare every last detail, but to allow for the spontaneous.

When I prepare I am conscious that I only have a few pieces of the jigsaw of worship – other people will complete the picture. This is a tension, because I would feel more comfortable beforehand if I had every element, but this does not allow room for God to utilise other members of his body to play their parts.

It is worth having an idea of songs that might be appropriate in response to the prophetic. Of course, you cannot prepare anything too specific as you do not know what the contribution will be, but it is helpful to have a list of the types of songs that might work. This is because, when you need to think up a song to respond to a specific contribution, it is all too easy for your mind to go blank and for you to find that you are unable to remember a suitable song. If you have a list with you of these types of songs this can help in those situations. Examples for this might be 'This is my desire' by Reuben Morgan or 'All I once held dear' by Graham Kendrick in response to the Lord asking us to be more devoted to him, or 'All around the world' by Paul Oakley, in response to prophecies about what the Lord will do among the nations. The permutations are endless, but it is helpful to have some ideas.

Scripture in worship

David had searched the Scriptures, as he refers to how the ark was carried in the time of Moses. As musicians we can easily get absorbed in our passion for playing and singing. Yet it is also vital for us to have a good grasp of God's word. Knowing the Bible helps us:

- *in our personal lives*
- *to lead worship in spirit and in truth* – to direct worship times into the truth of the Bible, preventing us from straying into error
- *as we quote Scripture in the worship times* to add content and weight to them
- *resist the attacks of the enemy*, who tempts us to sin, doubt and fear.

I have found it helpful to go through a concordance or a topical Bible and look at Scriptures relating to my theme. For example, in the example above about using Psalm 103:13 I might look up certain verses about God as Father and his love for us. I might write these down and have them near me during the worship to add additional scriptural truth to the worship time. Even if I don't use them, studying God's word helps me to align myself with Scripture's message as I come to lead.

Being practically prepared

The restoration of the ark to Jerusalem required a great deal of practical preparation. David had to organise priests, musicians, doorkeepers and soldiers, and even caterers to provide the bread and cakes referred to in 1 Chronicles 16:2! Leading a worship time doesn't usually just require you to turn up, but also to organise a number of things. These might include:

- *liaising with church leadership*
- *organising a band/PA rota*
- *confirming with your band/sound engineers that they will be there*

- *rehearsing the band*
- *providing the band with song lists and music*
- *ensuring all the songs are on the song projector/OHP.*

These are less glamorous than actually leading the meeting but are very important! The more I am involved in worship the more I become certain that effective administration is one of the core competences of worship leaders! The more organised I am before the day of the meeting, the less stressful the day itself becomes. I have been through disorganised phases where I have been frantically photocopying song lists and getting song words urgently put on OHPs, while the band are waiting to rehearse. This is an unhelpful background for leading God's people in worship, when we want to be as relaxed as possible, able to follow the leading of God's Holy Spirit.

If administration is not your strong point you may find it helpful to delegate aspects of it to someone else who is gifted in this area, thus freeing you to concentrate on leading worship.

Restoring the ark was a team effort

David could not have restored the ark on his own. It would have been impossible for one person to have carried it on the poles, and, as we have seen, there were many other tasks that needed to be completed for the day to be a success.

In the New Testament it is clear that worship times were not a 'one-man ministry', but a team effort.

> What then shall we say, brothers? When you come together, everyone has a hymn, or a word of instruction, a revelation, a tongue or an interpretation. All of these must be done for the strengthening of the church.
>
> *1 Corinthians 14:26*

1 Corinthians 12 also tells us that the Holy Spirit gives gifts to different members of the body of Christ.

The New Testament teaching is clear:

- the Holy Spirit gives gifts to members of the congregation when the church gathers together; and
- it is through *participation from various members of the body* that the church is strengthened.

It is interesting that while the Old Testament contains many details about musicians and how they were organised (please see Chapter 6), the New Testament is silent about these issues. The above passages from 1 Corinthians are two of only a few references to worship. I believe that this is because God wants us to focus on these passages. The distinctive hallmarks of new covenant worship are the priesthood of all believers and the Holy Spirit giving spiritual gifts to members of the congregation. Our worship should reflect these hallmarks and our concentration should be on what is truly unique about New Testament worship.

In worship, as at other times, the Holy Spirit is engaged in many activities such as guiding us into all truth and convicting of sin and righteousness, but these are not *explicitly* described as occurring in the specific context of worship. Instead, the New Testament explicitly states that the Holy Spirit's activity in church gatherings is giving spiritual gifts to the congregation. In order to experience New Testament worship we must therefore create an environment in which we allow the Holy Spirit to perform his work. I am all for musical excellence; however, this should not be at the expense of removing any opportunity for the spontaneous.

There is more detail about the practicalities of having different people participating in your time of worship in Appendix I at the end of this book. Contributions are like diesel oil: they can be messy to handle, but they provide fuel for worship times. Most of my best memories of worship times have been where a member of the congregation has contributed in a way that has caused the meeting to catch fire. Often, when I have led worship it has been a spontaneous song, a prophecy or a tongue and an interpretation from someone not in the band that has caused us to see breakthrough into another level of worship. It is always a little frightening for the worship leader to make room for contributions – it is much easier to sing one song after another and effectively keep control of the worship time, but the benefits far outweigh the risks.

The people couldn't contribute, but they did participate

In David's time it would not have been possible for every Israelite to individually contribute to the worship time by, say, praying out loud. At very large worship gatherings today it may also not be practical for most members of the congregation to contribute in this way.

However, the people of Israel were all fully involved in the occasion:

> So all Israel brought up the ark of the covenant of the Lord with shouts, with the sounding of rams' horns and trumpets, and of cymbals, and the playing of lyres and harps. *1 Chronicles 15:28*

In twenty-first-century western culture there is a danger that we are too used to being spectators. A great deal of entertainment is provided for us where we do not need to participate in any way. We just consume – and 'evaluate' (in reality, criticise!). When we are in a situation that calls for us to participate actively, such as church worship, we may find it difficult to be truly engaged and involved.

As worship leaders we can encourage those in our congregations to be participants, rather than consumers. I have found the following to be useful, when used at the right time, to engage the congregation:

* *Getting the congregation to read a Scripture together.* Reading a section from a psalm or a passage such as Ephesians 1:3-8 is a good way of engaging the congregation and also filling

their minds with truth at the beginning of the worship time.

- *Encouraging people to pray, applaud or shout together.*
- *Encouraging people to be expressive in their worship.* The Bible is full of physical actions in connection with worship – dancing, raising hands, bowing down, kneeling. It is usually counterproductive to instruct people to do these things. I find it works best to gently encourage people, in such a way that they feel free not to do what you suggest. Phrases such as 'you might want to dance', or 'some of you might want to kneel' may be ways of expressing this.

Bringing new songs to a meeting

In 1 Chronicles 16:7 it mentions a new song. We are not sure whether this was a song that had been written in advance of the occasion, specially for it, or one which was inspired during or after the event. All these types of creativity are valuable.

Introducing new songs helps to prevent our repertoire from becoming stale. If you teach a song that fits in with the theme you are leading on this can enhance a worship time. However, teaching new songs requires careful handling as there are some pitfalls. As people take time to get used to the song, this can have a deflating effect on the worship time. Some things that may help are:

- *Put new songs with familiar songs*

  If one new song might have a deflating effect on the worship time, then putting two songs together that the congregation is unfamiliar with almost certainly will! It is more helpful to the congregation to sandwich a new song between two songs they know well.

- *Get consensus on songs first*

  It is helpful to have a forum in which you can hear the opinions of other worship leaders in your church about songs before you teach them. If several worship leaders like a song then probably the congregation will like it as well, and also the other worship leaders are more likely to use the song you have taught. It is frustrating to go through the effort of teaching a new song in a worship time only for it never to be used again!

- *Don't start with a new song*

  If people need some help to get into worship, learning a new song usually isn't the best way to get them there. At some churches the band plays before the meeting starts, and this may be a good way of helping people to hear the song before the meeting starts. Similarly, if you play CDs beforehand, you could ensure that the new song you will teach is on the playlist – as long as you don't mind your version being compared with the one on the CD!

- *New songs at inter-church gatherings*

  Where Christians from a variety of different churches gather together everyone will feel slightly unsettled because they are not used to worshipping with each other and many will find it takes a little while to relax in the unfamiliar surroundings. It is usually helpful to try to sing songs that a reasonable proportion of the people will know, rather than something that very few are familiar with.

Teaching quality songs!

David's song was worth teaching and worth recording in Scripture. There are literally thousands of worship songs that you could teach in your church. Some of them are more worthwhile than others. How do we identify which songs will be successful? In Appendix III there is a 'Song Assessment Sheet' which may help you to do this. David's song contained the following features:

- ***The theme was apparent***

  David was writing about the greatness of God. If you read through the lyrics of a song and a theme is not immediately apparent then it may not be very successful. It is easy to produce the lyrics for a Christian worship song merely by amalgamating phrases of Scripture such as 'King of kings' and 'Lord of lords', which are wonderful, but can become clichés if used inappropriately.

- ***David's song was focused on who God is***

  This 'psalm' is full of description of God's greatness and, therefore, exhortations for the peoples of the nations to praise him. Sadly, many worship songs are heavily focused on us – the intention is to exhort us to praise the Lord, but unless they remind us of some of the many reasons why we should do so, it is unlikely to be effective. When we look at ourselves we are unlikely to want to praise the Lord – when we look at him we cannot avoid doing so! I am reminded of the schoolboy game of 'pulpit cricket'. You score a run every time the preacher says 'I' and lose a wicket every time he or she mentions God. If at the end of the sermon the score is 92 for 4 you know where the preacher's heart really lies! If the song is more focused on us rather than the Lord it is unlikely to be successful.

- ***David's song was focused on what God has done***

  Again, there are so many reasons for us to praise the Lord. A song that sets out some of these reasons will help your congregation to praise him. The truth sets us free. When we are reminded of God's character and all that he has done it liberates us in worship.

Spontaneous songs

You may find that during a worship time someone feels inspired to sing a song, either one that is completely spontaneous, or one that they have prepared earlier and they believe is appropriate for that meeting. This can really enhance the worship time. It is important that the band is highly sensitive at this point. They must play sufficiently quietly that the words of the songs are audible, but also they must pick up on the direction or flavour of the song. If the singer is exhorting the people to praise the Lord joyfully, it is important to have a suitable rhythm being played, without drowning the singer.

It's great to have an environment in which people can be creative and can take risks in bringing contributions. First of all, we should have a culture in our churches where we allow people to take risks and make mistakes. When people step out on a limb and, say, try to bring a spontaneous song, it's good to encourage them, even if the end result isn't very polished. I say to our musicians that I'd rather they took a risk and it went wrong than they held back from trying something different. Second, we should create space where people can bring a song. I try to keep playing a simple chord sequence after some worship songs have finished in order to give our congregation an opportunity to step in.

Often people find it easier to bring spiritual gifts in smaller group settings, so it is good to have some contexts in which people can develop until they feel comfortable in a larger gathering.

Taking a lead in worship

David took a lead in being a worshipper. When we lead worship we should also worship God ourselves. This may sound obvious, but we can be so conscious of the part we need to play in singing, playing, ensuring the band is following the song correctly and that the congregation is engaged in worship, that we can become distracted.

David was a role model to the people in worship, dancing 'before the Lord with all his might' (2 Samuel 6:14). This was clearly not something he was doing for show, but was genuine. Sometimes I make a conscious effort to put aside all the distractions around me and focus my attention on the Lord. However, we still need to remember that we are leading the congregation and must be aware of how much they are engaged in worship, always considering how best we can help them move on to the next stage of worship.

I also believe that the Lord has called those of us who lead worship to be role models when someone else is leading worship. Whether we are leading the meeting or participating as a member of the congregation, are we also engaged 100 per cent, loving the Lord with all our mind, heart, soul and strength?

Worship is a lifestyle

The worship does not end after the procession has finished.

> David left Zadok the priest and his fellow priests before the tabernacle of the Lord at the high place in Gibeon to present burnt offereings to the Lord on the altar of burnt offering regularly, morning and evening.
>
> *1 Chronicles 16:39-40*

Worship is not just for meetings; it should be a 'morning and evening event' – part of our lifestyles. When we're leading worship our relationship with the Lord can become focused around the meetings that we lead. Our prayer lives can also end up concentrating on asking God to help us with meetings. When I first became a Christian I was overwhelmed with the fact that I now had a relationship with God – that the King of the universe wanted to have fellowship with me, whatever I was doing. When I stray from this it can result in me seeking God for his blessing on the activities I'm involved in rather than seeking him for himself. For any relationship to thrive it requires quality time devoted to it for its own sake.

Although we are married my relationship with my wife can become superficial if I do not ensure that I set aside time to be with her, listen to her and communicate my thoughts and feelings. I cannot make the excuse that I am too busy: my marriage is a priority. Like a marriage, we are bound to the Lord through a covenant, yet our relationship with God can become superficial unless we too devote time to be with him, listen to him and talk to him. As we have seen in Chapter 2, it is from an overflowing relationship with the Lord that we will minister God's love and grace to others.

Returning home to be a blessing to our families

Leading worship is absorbing and it can also be thoroughly exhausting. It is tempting after the meeting to review the worship time in our minds and reflect upon how much better it might have been if we had, say, started with a different song. While it is useful to analyse what went well and what was not successful so that we improve things next time, we can get sucked into a dangerous self-absorption. We can also feel so tired that we can sit around in a stupor for the rest of the day. David went home to bless his family (1 Chronicles 16:43). To me this implies that he consciously left behind the events of the day, and actively sought to spend quality time with his family. It is often our families who lose out. As worship leaders we can spend a lot of time preparing, rehearsing and playing, and then afterwards we are exhausted! God's desire is for us to be a blessing to our families – not just to the church. I generally find that if I spend quality time with my children it actually helps me to unwind better than if I 'crash out' in front of the TV!

Points to remember

- *David was spiritually prepared.* He sought the Lord privately. Time with the Lord is an essential part of worship leading.
- *David was practically prepared.* This is also an essential part of worship leading. The more organised we are the more relaxed we can be before the worship time.

- *Restoring the ark was a team effort.* When the New Testament talks about worship it refers to body ministry and spiritual gifts. We should embrace the biblical values of allowing contributions from the congregation where this is practically possible.

- *David brought a new song.* It is good to use new songs, both those written in advance of the occasion and spontaneous songs. However, new songs require careful handling.

- *David took the lead in being a worshipper.*

- *Worship is a lifestyle.* Worship did not end after the procession finished but continued 'regularly, morning and evening'. Our lifestyles should be full of worship – not just on Sunday mornings.

- *David returned home to bless his family.* Worship leading can be exhausting but let's make sure we don't shortchange our families, but actively seek to bless them with our time and involvement.

Questions for practical application

1. Think of a theme for worship. What songs immediately spring to mind that fit this theme? What categories is it helpful for you to assign songs to? What Scriptures would fit into this worship time?

2. What are the areas of practical preparation that you believe help make worship run smoothly? How do you rate your own administration? What are your strong and weak areas in this regard?

3. To what extent is there 'team' involvement in your church's worship? Is there a way of encouraging more involvement from others?

4. Think of new songs that have been taught in your church recently. Can you identify the features of a successful worship song?

5. David danced 'before the Lord with all his might'. If you lead worship do you feel you can concentrate on worshipping the Lord yourself? If others are leading would you say that you worship with all your might? What inhibits this from happening?

6. To what extent is worship part of your lifestyle?

7. What happens when you get home after you have been involved in a worship time? How can you ensure you bless your family?

CHAPTER 6

Building a worship team

After David became king, he became responsible for the administration of the kingdom. This included organising a team of musicians.

Leading worship and playing instruments requires certain skills. Organising a band requires others! As we analyse the characteristics of David's group of musicians in the book of Chronicles we receive insight as to how worship teams can be organised along godly principles.

It is important first of all to remember that David's prime goals in organising his kingdom were:

- to glorify God
- to bless God's people.

In structuring our music groups we must always bear these two principles in mind. Everything we do must be to glorify God and to bless his people – his church. There are many temptations that we face as we try to manage worship teams. These may include trying to order things to be most convenient and fulfilling for ourselves. We may be tempted to try to achieve musical excellence to make us look good rather than to serve God and his people.

Priests first

In 1 Chronicles 23 verse 3 we read that the musicians were part of a total of 38,000 Levites, the priests of Israel. We should understand that we, too, are priests first, musicians second. What do we mean by priests? A priest in the Old Testament was someone who was set apart, chosen by God, to live a life of devotion to the Lord.

When someone wants to join your worship group you must ask yourself whether they are a 'priest'. Do they have a genuine, ongoing relationship with the Lord and are they devoted to him? All of us are inconsistent in the level of our passion for God as we walk through the pressures of life and various trials, so we cannot expect perfection, or anything near it! However, your music group will to some degree set the temperature for your church's worship. The group has a responsibility to lead the congregation into worship. If your musicians are lukewarm in their spiritual life then it is unlikely that your worship times will be amazing encounters with God! 'A phenomenal musician, with no heart for God, will actually hinder the worship of God we seek to inspire' * (Bob Kauflin).

David was a worshipper – in private and in public. It is difficult to gauge people's private devotion to God, but over time you can see whether they are displaying the fruit of the Spirit referred to in Galatians 5:22-23. Some can be very gifted, both in terms of their natural abilities, and/or in receiving and bringing spiritual gifts. However, qualities such as love, joy, peace, patience, kindness and self-control only come from walking with the Lord consistently.

It may be very difficult for you to evaluate the level of a person's spiritual commitment, particularly in a large church, because you cannot know everyone well. It is helpful to take soundings from your leadership team and from others, e.g. the person's small group leader, to gain some insight. I would always consult our leadership team before inviting someone

---

* From *What to Look for in a Worship Musician* by Bob Kauflin, as published in the Internet series *Worship Matters*. © (2001) by Sovereign Grace Ministries, Gaithersburg, MD. Used with permission. Website: www.sovereigngraceministries.org.

to take part, even for a 'one-off', as they are so much more in touch with the spiritual well-being of church members than I am. Once I had watched an individual lead worship at a small gathering and observed that they had gifting in this area. I suggested to one of our leaders that this person should be given an opportunity to lead worship at our main gathering on a Sunday morning. The leader was less than enthusiastic! A few months later the person backslid for a number of years (although I am happy to say that they are now serving God again!). The leader clearly had more insight into this individual's relationship with God than I did!

While worship can be feigned, you can generally establish over time whether your potential musician is, like David, a public worshipper. Ideally those in the worship group should be those who set an example in the area of public worship as well as private devotion to the Lord.

It is best to pray for wisdom over whom you add into your worship team! The Lord knows the individual's attitude and knows the future. God may speak to you directly as to whether to involve them or not. Many of us find it difficult to say 'No' but by doing so now you are not condemning the person to a life of non-participation – there may be a better time later on.

When people ask you if they can be involved in the worship team you can feel under pressure. Again, I have always found it helpful to use leaders and some of our senior musicians as sounding boards so that I know my decision is not subjective, but shared.

One of my prayers is for a spirit of discernment. I have only occasionally known this. Some years ago two young men approached me – one asked to play in the worship team. It was clear that he was very gifted, but within my spirit I felt uneasy about including him. His friend, who did not play an instrument, struck me rather differently. I felt I could discern humility in him. I remember thinking 'I wish you played an instrument.' Sadly, the first young man has encountered some difficulties in his relationship with the Lord. The second, I am delighted to say, later took up playing an instrument and is now a key member of our music team and is a joy to work with!

As part of being a 'priest' it is also essential that the person is truly committed to the church. Difficulties can arise when the person's church involvement seems to be only in relation to the worship team. They do not attend meetings consistently when they are not playing.

If this is the case you will need to talk through the issue with them. If this remains a problem (and the individual may attend more meetings for a short time after your conversation and then revert to their previous pattern!) you will need to take further action. After consulting your church leadership team, it may be best to remove their playing opportunities for a short time to see where their heart really lies. I have always found this type of step very painful, but in the end you need to preserve the integrity of your group's devotion to the Lord.

There can also be difficulties if the person does not share the vision of the church leadership. They may be devoted to the Lord, a public and private worshipper, but tensions may result if they are not committed to the direction in which your church is moving.

1 Chronicles 25 gives us a number of principles that will help us in our organisation of worship groups. I have quoted excerpts from verses 1-8.

Set apart

Verse 1 states that the musicians were 'set apart'. Musicians must be devoted to the Lord: they must also be dedicated to worship. Playing in a church worship team requires commitment:

- of time to attend rehearsals and arrive early for meetings
- of time to practise their instrument at home.

Above all, what is required is an *attitude* of commitment.

This is helped if the individual experiences a sense of 'calling' to play music for the Lord. If they aren't willing to be devoted to the team then it is unlikely that their involvement will be a success. This can be difficult where the people concerned are committed to God and to the church but are involved in so many other areas of church life that they cannot give sufficient time and energy to the worship group. In these instances you and they will have to come to a decision regarding their involvement in the worship group, and, potentially, in other areas of church life!

'Accompanied by'

1 Chronicles 25:1 states that the ministry is *prophesying*: it is to be *accompanied by* music. Lest we musicians gain too great a sense of our own importance it is good to remember that the musicians were there to provide accompaniment to the prophetic message. The music is there to serve and support God's message, not for its own sake. Our role as musicians and worship leaders is to serve the proclamation of the gospel. The music we play is not an end in itself, or a performance. We are there to serve the church.

Trained and skilled in music for the Lord

1 Chronicles 25:7 tells us that 'all of [the musicians were] trained and skilled in music for the Lord'. 1 Chronicles 15:22 tells us that 'Kenaniah the head Levite was in charge of the singing; that was his responsibility because he was skilful at it.' Quite obviously, musical competence is an essential requirement! Poor playing does not glorify the Lord!

There are three principles to draw out from the phrase 'trained and skilled in music':

1. Basic competence

There is obviously a need for all musicians to have sufficient basic competence. Playing music in a church setting may be difficult. At our church we have a huge repertoire of songs that might be used at a moment's notice, and musicians may be required to spontaneously transpose the song into a different key! The songs are in a variety of styles, requiring musicians to play, for example, rock, funk and hymns all at the same meeting! This is simply too difficult for some people at their current stage of musical development. However, I would far rather have a player of a basic standard who is truly devoted to the Lord, than a virtuoso who is not wholehearted in their relationship with God, or who is difficult to work with (please see the section on 'Bringing discipline' later)!

2. Continuing development

Many musicians (myself included) put in the greatest amount of practice during their teenage years. Some musicians can get 'stuck' and not continue to develop later in life, and their style of playing remains of the era when they first started playing! The best musicians I have worked with are those who have constantly sought to develop, by listening to and playing music of different types and styles. It is a challenge among the busyness of life to seek to develop our musical training but it does help us to serve our congregations better if we aim for continual improvement.

3. Music 'for the Lord'

The music that we play must be 'for the Lord.' To me, this means that our music must always be with a view to serving: serving God and his people by helping them to worship. It's tempting sometimes to play in such a way as to advertise our musical skills. As someone who loves playing electric guitar I can identify with the joke 'How many lead guitarists does it take to change a light bulb'? 'None – they just steal everyone else's light!' Sadly I can recognise my own tendency to want to play the riff that shows off my skills, rather than thinking more about what will bless the congregation. This does not mean that we shouldn't strive to excel and that solo parts aren't sometimes suitable. Our worship times have been enlivened by our guitarists or our trumpeter playing solos. But we do need to constantly challenge ourselves as to our motives and to be rigorous in the way we examine our own hearts. Bob Kauflin of Sovereign Grace Ministries puts it like this:

> An . . . attitude that should characterise those on our worship teams is humility, flowing from a fear of God. Something has gone tragically wrong when church musicians have a reputation for seeking the spotlight, comparing themselves to others, or needing to be handled with kid gloves. We have forgotten who we are before God, who 'esteems he who is humble and contrite in spirit' (Isaiah 66:2).*

Music for the Lord and for his people will also mean that we have to embrace musical compromise. A producer of many Christian albums once observed that, apart from weddings, church services are the only times when such a varied group of ages and backgrounds meet together and enjoy music. Across these there will be many musical tastes, and opinions on the optimum volume level will vary considerably. As musicians we have to be sensitive and try to serve all the people. Sometimes we can't play at the volume we'd like(!) and may also

---

* From *What to Look for in a Worship Musician* by Bob Kauflin, as published in the Internet series *Worship Matters*. © (2001) by Sovereign Grace Ministries, Gaithersburg, MD. Used with permission. Website: www.sovereigngraceministries.org.

have to soften some of our arrangements. I do not believe the Lord has any preference as to the style of music we should worship him with. It is the heart that is all-important. However, the style of music we play will probably be a compromise as we try to serve such a congregation of wide-ranging ages and tastes. Arrangements may have to be more 'middle of the road' than we'd like.

One of our musicians once remarked that we shouldn't look to church music to find our musical fulfilment; otherwise we'll always be trying to play songs that fit our preferred style, or to change arrangements to suit our preferences. He formed a band to play his favourite style of music at secular events which meant that when he came to play in worship he was already musically fulfilled: he was then happy to accept the compromises that inevitably occur when playing church worship music.

Under supervision

1 Chronicles 25:6 states that 'All these men were under the supervision of their fathers for the music of the temple of the Lord, with cymbals, lyres and harps, for the ministry at the house of God. Asaph, Jeduthun and Heman were under the supervision of the king.' The musicians were under the overall supervision of King David. This should be reflected on several levels. First, musicians must be devoted to Jesus, the King of kings. Second, as part of this, we must be in submission to our local leadership. What is submission? My personal definition is that it means throwing yourself 100 per cent behind someone else's vision. No doubt we share much of our leadership's vision, but there will be other times when we may think, 'I wouldn't do it that way.' Submission means devoting yourself to implementing what your leader wants to achieve. This does not mean that you can never make recommendations or voice criticism – but it should always be with the aim of assisting

your leadership to reach their goal, rather than as a way of achieving yours!

Many years ago on a Sunday morning I had just finished my final preparation for that day's worship when our pastor rang to say he wanted to change the order of the meeting and start with him preaching, followed by worship. He apologised for the short notice, but was confident that this was what the Lord wanted. My preparation would now be redundant, as I would have to choose songs to fit his sermon, rather than my theme! It was tempting to openly complain that I had already spent a lot of time on my preparation, or to pretend to be compliant but to sulk inwardly. In fact, I threw myself behind what my pastor wanted to achieve and am pleased that I did so as he had definitely been inspired by the Holy Sprit – the congregation responded to God in the worship time in a wonderful way.

Part of being under leadership's supervision means that our responsibility is to communicate our leadership's vision and priorities. In 1 Chronicles 16:7 it says:

> That day David first committed to Asaph and his associates this psalm of thanks to the Lord.

and then in verse 37:

> David left Asaph and his associates before the ark of the covenant of the Lord to minister there regularly, according to each day's requirements.

David is delegating to Asaph and the rest of the team the task of continuing David's ministry of praise and worship – by singing David's psalm and then continuing to minister. As musicians our role is to communicate our leadership's emphasis on elements of doctrine and ministry. In David's case he could not continue to minister personally because there were other calls on his time and so the work was delegated to

Asaph and the others. Many church leaders do not have the musical gifting to play instruments and sing, but our ministry is still delegated from them.

As such we have a great responsibility. We must make sure that we are in tune with what our leadership want to bring across. We need to listen to them, and to be receptive to what their current emphases are. We can then seek to continue their ministry through our own, rather than seeking to bring our own priorities.

The third level of being 'under supervision' is that David appointed men to serve under him. 1 Chronicles 25:6 tells us that 'Asaph, Jeduthun and Heman were under the supervision of the king', the others were 'under the supervision of their fathers'. It is practical to have a chain of command. Your church leadership will themselves appoint leaders to implement their vision – including musicians' leaders.

This may be easy for you, or problematic! You may find yourself submitting to someone who is less musically gifted than you, or you may find that they have a very different style and preference to you. We should be gracious towards them if they sometimes slip up on their administration or their handling of individuals (which we all do!).

At times like this it is good for us to remember David. Even though he was more gifted than Saul he submitted to him out of respect for Saul's role, rather than out of respect for Saul as an individual.

We must also be very careful that we do not find ourselves guilty of conceit. Philippians 2 urges us to have the same attitude as Jesus, and to 'do nothing out of selfish ambition or vain conceit, but in humility consider others better than your-selves' (verse 3). There have been a few times when I have felt that I should have been given greater opportunities to do certain things rather than others – only for the Lord to remind me of this verse! (Ouch!)

Rotas

It is interesting to note that in verse 8 it says that 'Young and old alike, teacher as well as student, cast lots for their duties.' I am not for a moment suggesting that this remains the way to organise your music group's 'duties'! However, it does illustrate that not everyone could play all the time. If your church is blessed with many musicians, you will have to have some form of 'rota' to share playing opportunities. However, I think this principle may be more relevant to those churches where there are few people available and musicians find themselves playing very frequently.

No musician should play every week. I have noticed over the years that where individuals have served every week in some capacity, either in music or in other areas, they 'burn out'. What begins as joyous service becomes a wearisome trudge. In the end the person has to relinquish their involvement either because they feel so jaded or, alternatively, their irritation with it becomes evident to others and does not actually help church life! While I would love to play music and lead worship every week, I have also noticed that if I do not have enough time off either I get obsessed with the music and lose my focus on the main goals of the church – preaching the gospel and making disciples – or I find music a chore and a burden, rather than a delight! It is interesting to note that the shared duties applied to 'young and old alike, teacher as well as student'. It is tempting for those of us in charge of music groups – the 'teachers' – to feel that we have to play all the time, but everyone else should have breaks. The principle of the Sabbath, that it is part of God's natural order to take a rest, should apply to our worship teams.

Even if you have only a few musicians it is best if they still have regular breaks. A good balance is two weeks on, two weeks off. To facilitate this you may need, on certain weeks, to have only one musician playing – a guitarist or keyboard player. It may seem undesirable in the short term, but will pay dividends over the long term.

It is not just important for the musicians themselves to have time off, but also for their families. My wife does not play in the music group, and I have to be sensitive that she does not feel a 'musician's widow', losing her husband to music! Many Sundays I leave for church early and am not with her during the worship. She really appreciates the Sundays when we travel to church together and I am beside her in the meeting. As musicians we must be sensitive to our spouses' feelings and as musicians' leaders we must allow people in our teams to put family first and not pressurise them to elevate music above their family's well-being.

David's musicians clearly worked as a team. Some must have been more gifted than others, but they considered themselves to be a team. 'Young and old alike . . . cast lots for their duties' – there were no superstars – the inexperienced and the experienced were each involved.

Responsible

Verse 8 of 1 Chronicles 25 refers to 'duties'. In 1 Chronicles 15:22 it states that 'Kenaniah the head Levite was in charge of the singing; that was his responsibility because he was skilful at it.'

If we believe we are called to music ministry this implies a certain amount of responsibility. This means ensuring that we put rehearsal and playing dates in our diaries and are quick to inform musicians' leaders when we are unable to attend – at the earliest possible stage. It means that we are willing to play at the less high-profile occasions as well as the larger settings.

The King James Version translates 'men' in 1 Chronicles 25:1 as 'workmen' and that is sometimes what we have to be. There are some musical commitments that appeal more to us than others, but our responsibility to the church is to fulfil them, just the same.

Sons and daughters

Verse 5 states that 'All these were sons of Heman the king's seer. They were given to him through the promises of God to exalt him. God gave Heman fourteen sons and three daughters.'

It is perhaps unlikely that many parents will play music with their children within the same worship group. However, one of the great delights in our music groups is being able to see young musicians introduced and discipled into mature musicians. In this way we can have musical 'sons and daughters'.

As a generalisation, I have found younger musicians highly enthusiastic, teachable and capable of coping with very steep learning curves.

Those in their teenage years and early twenties may well move away to different churches: at the time of writing, six of our young musicians have gone to University or have left to start churches in other areas in the last two years. But it has been a delight to send them, knowing that they have grown up as 'sons and daughters' in the time that they have been with us.

It is also interesting to note that the sons and daughters were given through the promises of God. As musicians' leaders we will often have to depend upon God's provision for enough musicians to meet the needs of our churches. On one occasion I was worrying about whether we would have enough musicians, only to hear the Lord clearly reminding me of the verse in Philippians 4:19: 'my God will meet all your needs according to his glorious riches in Christ Jesus.'

A 'son or daughter' implies to me someone who is willing to learn, someone who is 'teachable'. The best musicians I have worked with have been those who are receptive to instruction and guidance, willing to try new things and to try to play in ways that fit in with the group, rather than merely continue in their own style. Those who have just started playing in worship are frequently the most adaptable and receptive. However, I have had the privilege of working with some highly experienced musicians who remain fresh in attitude and approach despite the fact that they have been playing for a long time.

Some practical tips

The artistic temperament

Some time ago I attended a seminar with several other leaders of worship teams. When it was time for questions at the end someone asked, 'What should we do about the artistic temperament?' There was a murmur of agreement around the room. It was clearly a common problem! What do we mean by the 'artistic temperament'?

Before we answer this let me say that within your music group you may find that some of your team are highly sensitive people. Musicians' sensitivity is a gift from God, which helps them to react to the ebb and flow of worship during meetings. The flip side is that this sometimes means that their confidence may be fragile: you have to tread carefully in making any criticisms of their playing lest you destroy their confidence if you recommend any adjustments.

I have also worked with musicians who set such high standards for their own playing that they get extremely frustrated with themselves if they do not play to their own (very high) level of expectation. While this may be unhealthy self-absorption, in itself it does not create too many difficulties (although once one of our drummers became so frustrated with himself he walked out of the rehearsal for a few minutes, which made practising rather difficult!).

I have also found over the years that sometimes under the pressure of the situations we are in (for example we're all getting frustrated that the PA isn't working), we can say harsh things to one another in the heat of the moment. While this is not what the Lord desires, the reality is that, in moments of pressure, we may occasionally say things we regret. It is important that we are humble enough to reflect later upon our actions and put things right by apologising to those we have offended; and we must be receptive if others remark that we have said something harsh to them.

The Bible says that 'love covers over a multitude of sins' (1 Peter 4:8). When you have a good relationship with someone and you each know that your underlying attitude is to support one another, then the odd harsh word can be overlooked. We need at all times to be gracious to each other – not just in what we say, but in how we receive what others say.

However, it is unacceptable if an individual says harsh things, but does not apologise for (and seek to amend) his or her behaviour, even after you or others have sought to bring correction to them.

So – what do we mean by the 'artistic temperament'? I think this is where this 'sensitivity' is so extreme that the person becomes difficult to work with. For example:

- *Where musicians become unteachable*
  They believe so greatly in their own abilities and their own playing that they are resistant to any direction from the musicians' leader.

- *Where musicians are very critical*
  This may be of other musicians who are less gifted than themselves. Alternatively they may make critical comments of other people, including church leadership, that make everyone wince! It may also be that these same people take offence very easily themselves and expect to be handled with 'kid gloves'!

It is tempting to allow someone who is gifted more leeway over issues of character and behaviour on the grounds that they are 'artistes'. However, we should not lower our standards. If someone is causing disruption in the group, or is difficult to work with, then discipline will be needed.

Bringing discipline

Often within music groups a little correction here and there is fairly easy and painless. A brief word about someone's punctuality or personal administration in terms of writing down rehearsal dates can be said, privately, without many problems. It is important to keep your band up to the mark quietly and discreetly.

However, there will be other occasions when you may need to take a stronger line than merely a gentle word of correction. It may be that a few mild words have been unsuccessful, or perhaps their behaviour is sufficiently serious to warrant firmer action. This may well apply to those who act in the ways I have set out above.

Most people do not enjoy confrontation. You would be unusual if you do! Personally I go through sleepless nights worrying about such situations when they are brewing! However, there will inevitably be times when you need to exert discipline for the good of the group. I am pleased to say that over fifteen years of leading the music group at our church I have only needed to do this on a handful of occasions! Here are a few thoughts based on my own (painful) experience.

- *Always chat through the issues with your leadership team*
  They will have a wider perspective on the issues within the music group and will also have other insights regarding the person concerned. They will also understand your own personality and handling of the situation, and may identify areas that you could have improved upon! Make sure that any action is agreed with your leadership team prior to you taking it.

- *Make sure the issue you refer to doesn't come 'out of the blue'*
  If you are asking someone to stop playing it should not be on an issue that you have not raised with them before. You should raise it at an early stage so that they know that their

bchaviour is a problem and have an opportunity to change. The only exceptions to this would be something very grave, such as serious sin issues, or where their attitude has been so inharmonious that your team is cowering at the thought of working with the individual. In these instances immediate corrective action is required.

- *Talk it through with the person face to face*

  While the conversation will be uncomfortable, emails, letters, and even phone calls are unsatisfactory means of communication for this type of news. Our apprehension about such conversations is often made worse by the fact that the people who are difficult to work with may be rather intimidating, and may have 'volcanic' temperaments – you never know when they're going to erupt! But we must be courageous and meet with the individual. However, it may be wise to take someone else with you. They should be someone in leadership or a senior member of the music group. This may take some of the heat out of the situation, give you invaluable moral support, and they also may be able to reinforce the points you are making, demonstrating to the person that this is not something that only you feel is an issue.

- *Do not give a 'return' date*

  If you are asking someone to step down from the worship group my experience is that it is unwise to specify a date when they can come back to playing. While it seems more palatable at the time to give them a date when they can return rather than ask them to stop playing indefinitely, you are then left with the prospect of the person coming back into the group when they may not have responded to the issue(s) you have raised. You are far better to give no undertaking or timescales. It also means that the person concerned knows that they are expected to change in some way before they can return. However, it may be helpful to set a future date to review the person's progress with them so that they know there is a route back.

A very difficult aspect of discipline is how you communicate what has happened to the rest of the group. You do not wish to publicise the person's shortcomings, but, if the person has been asked to leave the team, the others will need to know that they have stopped playing. It will also save your band from unwittingly asking the person why they aren't now making appearances in the group! This is immensely difficult. It may be best to gather your team together and speak to them, discreetly.

Building a band

A band is a team, but many church groups don't play like it! My football playing days are long behind me, but I remember needing to know what my role as right-back was and stick to it. My teammates would be frustrated with me if they were looking for me to pass to them on the right-hand side of the pitch only to find that I'd gone over to the left!

In a band each member has a team role, but you frequently find musicians not fulfilling their roles or duplicating others'.

A classic example of this is guitars and keyboards. They can often end up occupying the same musical space and the result is that the sound becomes cluttered. Many keyboard players have been trained as pianists, where they are used to playing on their own. They have been trained to play the melody and chords in their right hand, and the bass in their left. But in a band a bass player is playing the bass, a guitarist the chords and the singers are providing the melody. Consequently the keyboards have to find space elsewhere, perhaps by providing some lead piano at the top end, or else some 'light and shade' – a 'pad' string sound or organ and adding vibrato from time to time for effect. Alternatively, guitarists may need to alter their playing style to stop them crowding out the keyboard player's space. They may need to leave the chords to the keyboard, and pick single notes rhythmically or play lead.

Another example could be lead instruments (e.g. flutes, lead guitars) playing so much that they crowd out the vocals. It is best to play in the pauses between vocal lines, rather then all the way through. Even then, playing in every gap may be an example of the law of diminishing returns!

'Less is more'

As musicians it is hard to grasp that sometimes we actually add more to the sound by not playing all the time! We will then be adding variation when we come in or drop out rather than have a monotonous arrangement that is cluttered with many instruments.

Sometimes musicians feel that if they are in the band they have to justify their existence by playing all the time – if they stop they feel insecure. Alternatively, sometimes they may not be listening enough to the overall sound of the band to realise that by playing they are crowding the sound.

A general rule is that the bigger the band, the less the individual members should play. If everyone plays all the time, we clutter up the sound. We have to listen out for each other and give each other space.

Running rehearsals

Over the years I have tried many different approaches in terms of running rehearsals. Here are some thoughts:

- ***Book people's diaries at an early stage***

  I try to plan about three months at a time, including the Sunday morning rota and rehearsal dates. Many of the people involved in church music will be very busy with other church duties, responsible jobs and family commitments. You will find the process runs much more smoothly if you get the dates out early, so that they are in everyone's diaries, and then they can let you know if they can't make it at an early stage. This includes booking the place where you will rehearse, and also getting someone to do the PA if this is necessary.

- *Remind everyone about the rehearsal*

  Despite giving out the dates, I have found it essential to remind people nearer the time. E-mail and text messaging are wonderful tools in this regard. I always ask our musicians to confirm their attendance.

- *Practise songs you are likely to play in worship*

  This sounds incredibly obvious, but requires discipline and forward planning! What I have found to be very successful is to prepare the worship time I will be leading *in advance* of the rehearsal, so that we can play the songs I plan to use at the meeting we are rehearsing for. Our rehearsals are generally on Monday to prepare for the following Sunday, which means that I have to prepare for the rehearsal at least a week ahead of the actual event. While I will not have a finalised list of songs, it is helpful to the musicians to rehearse at least some of the songs they will be playing and to work on the arrangements. The rehearsal is sometimes used as a test of whether the songs are appropriate. If a song doesn't sound good at the rehearsal, then I will sometimes (but not always) take this as guidance that it will not work that Sunday. I also look out for the musicians' reaction to the song – I have sometimes found their reaction is 'not this one again' – showing that a song has become stale! However, it's worth bearing in mind that sometimes we musicians love to play songs that are musically challenging, that may not necessarily be to the congregation's taste.

- *Have a (flexible) plan*

  There is nothing more frustrating for musicians than to give up an evening to attend a rehearsal that is badly prepared.

If everyone has confirmed attendance, the PA is set up and you have a plan of what you will be doing, you are far more likely to find your musicians to be enthusiastic rehearsers. I will write down a list of songs to practise, and the probable order that we will play them; however, flexibility is essential. If your drummer's late, you may find that playing the rocky song first isn't appropriate – you might be better playing the worshipful hymn. While some musicians are setting up you might want to work on some vocal harmonies for the singers – or even allow the singers to arrive slightly later than the rest of the group, as they have no equipment to set up.

- *Spend time worshipping and praying together*
  This reminds everyone (including myself) of the real reason why we're playing, and that everything we do must be with the sole aim of glorifying Jesus. It's good to take your eyes off the rehearsal for a while to focus on the Lord. Worshipping and praying together brings unity of heart and purpose to your band.

- *Leave room for the spontaneous*
  It is good sometimes to keep playing the chord sequence of a song and improvise around it. If you're looking for freedom and spontaneity during your worship meetings it is good to establish an environment in your rehearsals where your musicians can experiment and make mistakes – where your guitarist can try out a solo and the drummer a new beat. In planning a rehearsal I will try to identify some songs where we can continue with the chord sequence and allow the musicians to improvise and the singers to bring spontaneous songs if they feel it is appropriate to do so.

- *Allow the team to flesh out the bones of your arrangements*
  It's good to come to a rehearsal having thought through what the individual instruments will do in a particular

song. This might involve you working out some individual parts, or bringing a CD to the rehearsal to give your musicians some idea of how the song goes. However, once the group is working well together you can give them more freedom to develop the arrangements. One of my greatest pleasures with the band I usually work with is to see them take an idea and develop it. I retain the power of veto in case the ideas run away with themselves, but church life generally works best with the involvement of a team, and music is no exception.

Organising your worship group

You will almost certainly need to organise your group into teams. I have found that if musicians play together regularly, and have some compatibility, then 'chemistry' can develop that makes the band sound greater than the sum of its parts. Only you will know exactly how to best put your group into individual teams, but here again are some thoughts.

- *Prayer* – It is helpful to pray for your group and for you to have wisdom on how to organise it. Only the Lord knows the future.

- *Consultation* – Ask your leadership team what they think. While most will probably not be musicians, they will have some good insights. Also ask your senior musicians what combinations will work best, although all of us want to play with the best musicians all of the time!

- *Observe the merits of different combinations* – For example I have noticed that some combinations of drummers and bass players have gelled, others have not. This is the foundation of the music group, and should be put together with particular care.

- *Adopt different styles* – We have a violinist and flautist in our group. However, if they play with the 'rockier' members of the team, they can get drowned out. While this sort of situation calls for us to 'submit to one another' (Ephesians 5:21), we have sometimes put the more 'classical' instruments in a lighter sounding band which then gives them more freedom, and allows the rockier band to play the arrangements that suit those musicians' styles best.

- *Different levels of commitment* – Rehearsing worship songs is a classic example of the '80/20' rule. Getting the song to sound OK (80 per cent right) takes only 20 per cent of the time. It takes 80 per cent of the time to get the last 20 per cent right. For example, the atmospheric 'intro', the slick ending, and, more than anything else, analysing the arrangement in detail. This would include ensuring that the bass and drums are properly locked in a groove together, the keyboard and guitar aren't occupying the same musical space, and ensuring the vocal harmonies don't clash with each other or with other instruments. You may find that some members of your team are keener than others to work on the detail of a song. Some in your group may be so enthusiastic they would like a rehearsal every week. Others may have so many other commitments that they find making the time available to rehearse very difficult. You may wish to split your overall group into bands: some that work hard rehearsing arrangements and others where the commitment required is less. Alternatively, you may decide that all your bands should be rehearsing frequently and that different levels of commitment result in inconsistency – once again this emphasises the need for prayer to receive wisdom.

Working with PA

PA is one of the most thankless tasks in church life. Generally, people only notice it when it goes wrong. If the sound is brilliant they tend to say 'the band was great' rather than 'the PA team got a great sound!' Yet working closely with our PA team

I can see that they spend hours working to get something right that the congregation can take for granted.

If the PA isn't working well prior to a meeting, musicians' stress levels tend to increase and sometimes this can lead to them expressing their frustration to the PA team who are doing their best to resolve the problems. It is very important that we appreciate our PA staff, and remember to thank them every time, regardless of whether it's been problematic or trouble-free, so that they know that we appreciate them. After all, without them we as musicians will not be heard and the worship will suffer.

It's also useful for musicians to learn as much as they can about how the PA works. It's good to learn at least enough to get the foldbacks working effectively enough so that you don't need PA people at rehearsals. The more you learn, the more you understand about the complexities and appreciate the difficulties your PA team work through.

Points to remember

- *David's musicians were 'priests' first.* All musicians in your team should display evidence of a personal relationship with the Lord.

- *David's musicians were set apart.* Music involves dedication. A sense of calling greatly helps to prioritise time.

- *Music is an accompaniment to the message, not an end in itself.*

- *David's team was trained and skilled in music for the Lord.* We need to have basic competence in our instruments – but that is just a beginning. We need to practise to serve our churches and to serve the Lord.

- *David's musicians were under the supervision of the king.* We are in submission to Jesus, the King of kings, our local church leadership and also to those whom our church leadership ask to lead our music groups.

- *Kenaniah had responsibility in David's music group.* Being a member of a worship team involves discipline and reliability.
- *David's team had 'sons and daughters'.* It is a wonderful aspect of church life when younger church members can be discipled by those who are more experienced.

Questions for personal application

1. What do you believe are the main features of a successful music team?

2. When you have observed someone running a rehearsal particularly well what were the features that made the session work?

3. Think of a worship song you particularly like. Mentally, arrange the song, considering each instrument in turn. How can you utilise the different instruments in your band without the sound becoming too cluttered?

CHAPTER 7

Songwriting

David was a remarkable songwriter. Some of his songs are so memorable that we are still using the words, some three thousand years later. With seventy-four of the 150 psalms described as being 'of David',* he is arguably the most successful worship songwriter of all time.

How did he do it? We will draw out some features from his songs to help us to be successful.

Why write songs?

There are excellent reasons for writing songs, as we will see from David's example. Some of these include:

- *Songs glorify God and encourage others to glorify him*
  There is no question that David's psalms glorify God. When we read words such as:

  > O Lord, our Lord, how majestic is your name in all the earth . . . When I consider your heavens, the work of your fingers, the moon and the stars, which you have set in place, what is man that you are mindful of him? *Psalm 8*

  how can our response be anything other than to join with David in worshipping our great Creator?

- *Songs express God's goodness to us on specific occasions*
  Some of David's psalms convey his thanks for specific

---

* See later paragraph regarding the phrase 'of David'.

situations when God delivered him. Some commentators think that Psalm 65 was a song written specifically to thank God on behalf of the people for answering prayer, perhaps after the end of the three-year famine in 2 Samuel 21:1-4. You may find that God inspires songwriters in your congregation to write songs that specifically apply to your church and its current situation.

- *Songs help us understand doctrine*
  The psalms do not *teach* doctrine: they are poetry and should be read in this context; however, they can help us to *understand* doctrine. For example, the beautiful Psalm 139 helps us to understand God's omnipresence in a personal way.

- *Songs encourage us*
  David's own personal experience of God's deliverance when he was being pursued by his son, Absalom, comes across vividly in Psalm 3 ('But you are a shield around me, O Lord'). We can take these words to heart because we know that they are true, thanks to David's record of his experiences through song.

- *Songs of passion for God and an intimate relationship with him challenge us*
  The intimacy of David's relationship with God, e.g. Psalm 63, serves as a challenge to us to reach a similar level of relationship with him.

Furthermore:

God deserves praise in every possible way

In Revelation 7 we read of 'a great multitude that no one could count, from every nation, tribe, people and language' praising God (verse 9). Our God is magnificent. It is only when all the peoples of the world praise him with all the richness of worship being expressed in all the languages of the earth and with influences from every culture that we will even approach the worship that he deserves. Each new song that is written is a new expression of praise to God, adding to the collage of worship, past and present, across the globe that adds to the picture that will only be completed in heaven.

The Holy Spirit is an inexhaustible source of creativity

In Psalm 40 David writes that the Lord 'put a new song in my mouth, a hymn of praise to our God'. It is not David who is the source of the inspiration, but the Lord himself. The Holy Spirit, who brings freshness to our worship, also wants to inspire us with new songs. We can come to God in faith that he will give us creativity.

What makes a great song?

What are the chief elements of a great song? As a worship leader always on the lookout for songs that will inspire the congregation, and also an occasional songwriter, I would identify the following features:

A song with a theme

There are many worship songs I listen to that do not have an identifiable theme. The Bible is so full of wonderful, lyrical phrases, such as 'Lord of lords' and 'King of kings', that it is very easy simply to amalgamate these together without following a coherent path. Psalm 139 is centred on a single theme – the personal care of an omnipresent God from the perspective of an individual. A single theme does not mean a single idea – many people would remember that Psalm 23 compares God to a shepherd; however, this is not the whole story. The second section of the psalm, from verse 5, moves on to a different image – that of the banqueting table. The overall theme is God's lavish love and goodness to us, using two different images. We can use different images within a song – but we should incorporate them within a single theme.

It is easy to fall into the trap of trying to include the whole gospel within a single song. While there are a few exceptions where this works, generally it is better to narrow the scope of your song.

When I write a song a test I apply is whether I can summarise its message in a single sentence. If I cannot do this then it may be that the song does not have a coherent theme.

Songs about God's character and what he has done

David's songs inspire us because they remind us of who God is and what he has done. For example, Psalm 103 sets out some of the benefits of being in relationship with the Lord:

> He forgives all my sins and heals all my diseases;
> he redeems my life from the pit and crowns me with
>   love and compassion.
> He satisfies my desires with good things, so that my
>   youth is renewed like the eagle's.   *Psalm 103:3-5*

I find that the songs that inspire me to worship speak of who our Lord is, and the amazing things he has done and continues to do.

There is a disturbing trend in worship songs of centring on what *we* will do – e.g. '*I* will praise you, *I* will lift up your name', without giving any solid reasons why God deserves our praise. If we sing too many songs like this our worship becomes devoid of content. Songs like this may work better toward the end of a worship time. Once we have reminded ourselves of the multitude of reasons why God deserves our praise, we can then sing songs of response to this. Try to avoid having too much of 'I' or 'We' as the *subject* of the sentences in your songs – '*I* will worship' – and make sure the song is focused on God, not on us. A middle way is to write about what the Lord has done in, say, the verses, then in the chorus say how 'I' or 'We' will respond in praise.

Lyrics everyone can identify with

The success of the idea of 'The Lord's my shepherd' is that it is timeless and has universal appeal. Everyone can relate to the theme across different cultures and ages. We will impair the effectiveness of our songs if we use language that others cannot relate to. For example, if our song is too personal we will diminish its impact. Furthermore, if you use 'in' phrases that are, say, only spoken by young people then older members of your congregation may find it difficult to relate to the song. A further complaint I hear from our congregation is where the language could be that of romance rather than of worship and it is not immediately apparent that the Lord is the object of adoration in the song.

Songs from 'the secret place'

It is clear from David's songs that he was inspired by his own times of worship. Psalm 8 must surely have been the result of David worshipping the Lord. Certainly some of my most successful songs have come out of personal worship in which I felt inspired. As we spend time with the Source of creativity he will inspire us.

Songs from personal experience

Our songs have more impact if they are based on experience. David's songs are personal, which is why we still feel the impact of those songs.

Singing songs written by members of your congregation may also convey a sense of shared personal experience if they reflect a particular season your church is going through and convey an appropriate message relating to this. This will be relevant to everyone in your church. You can also try to write songs that reflect the teaching your church is receiving from your leadership team, as this will help your congregation to take hold of what your leaders are trying to express.

Many of David's psalms relate to difficult times he was going through, where he is pouring his heart out to God in his desire for vindication and deliverance. These are a great encouragement to us when we are going through difficult times. However, if you ask people in your congregation which are their favourite psalms it will probably be those that speak of God's love and greatness. Hence our songs will have more appeal if we write on these themes. While the songs you write about your own difficulties and desire for God's deliverance are valid and are probably therapeutic to you in expressing your anguish, songs that encourage everyone about God's goodness, love and faithfulness will probably appeal more to your congregation!

Songs with form

There is a saying that works of art are the result of 10 per cent inspiration and 90 per cent perspiration. While David's songs are obviously the products of divine inspiration, they also required songwriting craftsmanship. As we are reading the psalms in translation from the Hebrew it is perhaps difficult to appreciate this, but many of David's psalms are in the form of acrostics, so he would have had to apply considerable discipline to start each line with a prescribed letter of the Hebrew alphabet.

A great musician and songwriter I used to work with said that people would sometimes give him songs they'd written and say, 'God's given me this song.' His reaction on hearing the songs was to think – 'God's not a very good songwriter'! What had really happened was that the songwriter believed they were inspired, but had not been able to apply sufficient craft to make the song successful. We may have moments of genuine inspiration from God, but unless we learn the craft of songwriting and work hard on our initial ideas we will not produce a song that others will want to sing.

There are several areas in which we need to apply song-writing craft.

Lyrics must fit the tune

This may sound obvious, but some songs display weakness in this area. The *emphasis* of the words needs to fit the tune. If any words in your song sound unnatural when they are sung, you probably need to re-write them! Each word should sound natural when it is sung.

Consistent length of lyrics

Make things easy for your congregation by making your lines consistent. If the first line of the first verse contains seven syllables, then the first line of your second verse should be exactly the same length. Songs by pop and rock groups do not follow this discipline, because they don't need to – the singer will make minor adjustments to the timing of each verse, but if you're writing a worship song it will, hopefully, be sung by hundreds of people together. Songs will be more successful if your congregation find them easy to learn. Again, if a musical phrase is repeated – say on the second and fourth line of each verse, then it is better if both the number of syllables and the pattern of emphasis are consistent in these lines.

Lyrics must contain sound doctrine

While the psalms, and our worship songs, are poetry, this does not excuse sloppy doctrine. Sometimes I read the lyrics of worship songs and find individual lines spoil the song because they are not theologically sound. Often I think I know what the author meant, but if you take the line at face value it is not biblical. While songs are not sermons, if you listen to members of your congregation or small group pray, you'll see that sometimes people take the words of songs as if they are doctrine! With my own songs I believe I should be able to justify every line with a verse of Scripture. Fitting the line in with the tune may mean it can't be a direct quotation from the Bible, but it must be doctrinally sound. Jesus said that 'true worshippers will worship the Father in spirit and truth' (John 4:23). If we are to help our congregation to be the true worshippers the Father seeks, our songs must be full of scriptural truth.

Blend lyrics sympathetically with the melody

Endeavour to blend sympathetically the shape of the melody and the meaning of the words. For example, don't set inconsequential words such as 'and' as the climactic point of the melody. Similarly, phrases such as 'You lift me up' are not effective in the lower register! Melody facilitates the emotion the lyrics are expressing and can give particular emphasis to words that then come alive with meaning.

Range

As a musician, it is likely that your vocal range is wider than the average member of your congregation. Many people only have a comfortable range of about one and a half octaves. If your song is any wider in range than just over an octave you will probably need to simplify it. Songs should be geared to your congregation's range, and not to yours! You will find that on many worship albums the songs are written around the singer's best range and keys and you may well have to make adjustments to the keys to suit your congregation. Sadly, the range of some songs is too wide to be sung by a congregation – lower the song to get the top note within the congregational 'ceiling' and the lowest part of the song is too low for the average voice!

Sometimes I will lower the key of a song for a meeting in someone's home as a small group can sometimes struggle with a range that a congregation is quite comfortable with on a Sunday morning when they are being led by a band and singers. Typically regard D as the top of the range but, particularly in sustained passages, women may prefer to sing no higher than C above middle C.

Keys

Songs sound different when you play them in alternative keys. As a general rule, keys with sharps sound 'bright', while keys with flats sound 'mellow'. Jazz is often in keys with flats. So if you write a song and then want to raise or lower it, you'll find that the character of the song changes. If you write a song in A, for example, you'll lose some of its brightness if you move it into Bb or C (C is fairly neutral, having no sharps or flats). Moving it into B will brighten it. Of course you also have to think about the voicing of the instruments – some of your musicians may find it difficult playing songs in keys with lots of flats and sharps, particularly if they play a transposing instrument such as the trumpet. Some keys may be more difficult for guitarists and bassists – they may not be able to use open strings for 'riffs' or, for the guitarists, they may not be able to play certain chord voicings. With the band I play with regularly if we are in any doubt we will experiment by trying a song in alternative keys. To facilitate this you may have to help your musicians by writing out the song in different keys.

'Hooks'

When you hear a song on the radio for the first time the 'hook' is the catchy bit you remember when the song finishes. (No, not every song has one!)

You will greatly enhance your song if you have at least one hook. Many worship songs do not have any, but you will help your song if you work on a memorable chorus line. Good examples of hooks from worship songwriters are 'I could sing of your love forever' by Delirious and 'Beautiful One' by Tim Hughes. If your song has a hook your congregation may remember it enough to sing it during the week. If the 'hook' they are singing is Scripture it will help them to meditate on biblical truth. Imagine sending everyone home from your meeting singing something like 'Nothing shall separate us from the love of Christ' in their cars!

Simplicity

It is best to keep songs simple! Your song will (hopefully) be sung by a large congregation of people. En masse, they will not find songs that have difficult intervals, complicated tunes, or modulations between keys easy to pick up. You may also find that they simplify the timing. If your tune is reliant on syncopation you may find that your song is radically different when the whole congregation is singing it! A while ago, when the congregation was learning one of my songs for the first time, I could hear one lady in the congregation singing the tune, very loudly, with all the syncopation removed! It was a lesson for me and I stopped using the song because I did not feel that it was suitable for a congregation!

Songs that sound as if the words have had to be shoe-horned into each line are another area where you will not be helping your congregation. One of the faults of my early days of songwriting was trying to cram too many words into each line. It's better to be economical!

Structure

As mentioned earlier, some of David's psalms are in a particular form, such as A, B, C, B, A. Every song has a format. A common one for today's worship songs is:

A1   First verse
A2   Second verse
B1   Chorus
A3   Third verse
B2   Chorus
C   Bridge
B3   Chorus

You must choose the most suitable format for your song. However, here are some points to remember:

- Too many different sections may make the songs difficult for a congregation to pick up.

- Make sure all the sections fit together well. Your verse and chorus may be good tunes in their own right, but may not fit together particularly well. Some bridges can sound as if they were tacked onto the song rather than fitting in. You are better to defer finishing the song until you get another idea rather than trying to weld together incompatible sections!

If you are interested in studying songwriting in more detail there are a number of books dealing exclusively with the subject. 'God Songs' by Paul Baloche and Jimmy & Carol Owens may be particularly useful for those seeking to write worship songs.

Finding out if your song is any good!

When we create anything we feel excited about what we have achieved, but we also feel vulnerable, because we have put something of ourselves into our work. Therefore we play our material to others with trepidation in case they are critical. However, if we are to grow as songwriters we need to seek honest feedback.

Many of the people we play our songs to will want to encourage us, but may not be honest enough to tell us what they really think. Find those whose opinion you trust and who will give you a true evaluation of your song. A panel of 'yes' men or women will not ultimately help you to develop.

I use a number of filters to test my songs.

- *My wife* – She is a very helpful critic. With one song I felt very pleased at what I had produced and had written four verses that I thought were equally good, but believed that four was one too many for the song. I asked her to say which three she thought were best. To my surprise she thought that the lyrics overall were not consistent in their theme and were below the standard of some of my other songs. The tune was also too complicated in one part. After initially feeling upset by this, I realised she was right, worked hard on simplifying the tune and tightening the lyrics and produced one of my best songs – her critique was invaluable.

- *The band* – It's great to try a song with your band, even if it's not finished. You will get a much better idea of what it will ultimately sound like, and they have a chance to influence the style and development of the song. I have asked my band to be honest with me about the quality of my songs. One song I played was greeted with complete silence. This was not a quietness due to reverent awe at the presence of the Lord – this was different! They were trying to work out who would be first to tell me it was a flop! Eventually a member of the band gave a truly honest opinion on the song in no uncertain terms – as he hadn't heard it was one of mine! He apologised after he realised I was the composer, but in fact I was grateful that he said what he really thought, rather than just trying to please me. I would hate to use a song in worship simply because no one in the band had told me the truth – and everyone in the congregation was cringing when they came to sing it! We need to encourage honesty.

  The band also provides great feedback on different parts of the song. They will tell me which parts of the song are easy to sing and which they find hard to pick up. With one song they sang the chorus differently than I'd written it because they'd 'heard it' in a different way. Their way was better than mine, so I changed the song! I will provide the band with a blueprint of an idea of the 'groove' of the song, but they may make some adjustments.

- *The congregation* – Sometimes it's difficult to tell whether a congregation like a new song – they may take a while to pick it up. However, I will ask a few people what they think of any new song I teach. I do not generally put my name on my songs when we sing them at church – that way I get truly honest feedback! I once asked one of our leaders about a song I'd taught that morning and he, not knowing it was mine, said, 'It's a bit forgettable'! I was grateful for his honesty and dropped the song immediately afterwards – looking back objectively I now realise he was right! On the other hand I've had people asking me about other songs – 'Where did that come from? It's great!' – the fact they hadn't realised it was home-grown makes their praise all the sweeter!

Where people know that I've written the song I've taken anything less than wholehearted praise to mean that they didn't really like it. Most Christians like to be positive – so if they're not that enthusiastic it probably means they don't like your song! However, a lack of feedback does not necessarily mean people did not like the song. You may need to ask people for comments.

Submitting your song for evaluation

Ensure that when you present a song to other people you are giving them permission not to like it – to be honest in their views. Also be cautious about being pushy and hustling to get your songs used in worship times. As a 'customer' of songs, I've found this type of attitude off-putting and counterproductive. I think the best method is to record your songs – it doesn't have to be an elaborate production – just voice and either guitar or keyboard onto a tape is sufficient. If the song is good it will shine out. Leave it with your worship leaders to listen to for a while. I find that there are many songs I am unimpressed with on the first listen, but which I come to love over time.

Some other thoughts

Originality

David's songs weren't always original. Psalm 68 borrows certain phrases from Numbers 10. It is unlikely that your song will be totally new in either lyrical or musical content – don't worry, you're in good company! However, do be careful that you haven't subconsciously plagiarised tunes from other people – it's so easy to do. I spoke with one well-known Christian songwriter who said that he'd once written what he thought was one of his best ever songs – only to realise the next day that the tune came from a Delirious track!

You may find that you can 'recycle' parts of your song. Perhaps, overall, the song you have written might not be good enough, but there may be bits of it you can rescue and re-use later. David sometimes repeats himself. Psalm 108 is composed of parts of two other psalms, 57 and 60! Perhaps he, too, was recycling his songs!

Some of David's songs were more memorable than others

David is probably the most successful worship songwriter of all time, yet some of his songs seem to be more memorable than others! Ask any member of your congregation which of David's psalms they can remember and they will probably identify Psalms 23, 139, 8, 51, 110, 3 and perhaps a few more, but essentially there are only a few that stick in people's minds.

The great songwriter Charles Wesley was remarkably prolific, writing over 8000 hymns during his life. Yet in the latest edition of *Hymns and Psalms* (the Methodist hymn book), only about 150 are included.

We can feel under pressure to produce successful songs consistently and then see ourselves as failures when we 'only' produce something that is 'quite good'. We should take encouragement from David that not every song we write will be a huge hit. If you produce only one song in your life that helps your congregation to respond in worship to the Lord then that will be a magnificent achievement.

As you've probably gathered, my 'hit rate' of songs I write is pretty low. For every ten songs I start on, 30 per cent fall by the wayside before I've played them to anyone else, 10 per cent after playing them to my wife, 20 per cent after I've played them to the band and a further 20 per cent get dropped after the first time I've taught them to our congregation. Consequently, only about two in every ten songs I write ever become 'regulars'. If I get two 'hits' a year, I'm doing well.

Creating a culture in which songwriting can thrive

It is interesting to note that members of David's music team were also songwriters – Asaph, one of the team leaders, wrote some of the psalms, as did the sons of Korah. David obviously developed an environment in which creativity could thrive. If you're a musicians' leader make sure you give opportunities for people to practise playing songs they have written with the band. The songs may not be brilliant, but it is important to let them see what the song sounds like with the band, and to get feedback from them. If you're a worship leader, give thought to using homegrown songs. As long as they are reasonably good you will be encouraging the development of in-house talent even if it's some way from being the finished article.

'Of David'

Many of the psalms have the inscription 'of David' above them.

The NIV Study Bible* comments:

---

* Hodder & Stoughton, 1987, p. 765.

> As for Davidic authorship, there can be little doubt that the Psalter contains Psalms, composed by that noted singer and musician and there was at one time a 'Davidic' Psalter. This, however, may also have included Psalms written about David, or concerning one of the later Davidic kings, or even Psalms written in the manner of those he composed.

We could get ourselves into a long debate about whether the psalms were actually written by King David himself or not. However, if David set in place a tradition of songwriting where others took on his style and developed their own songs – wasn't that also a great achievement? The best thing we can do for our churches is to create an environment in which people can be inspired by the Holy Spirit to craft songs that will enrich our worship.

Recognition

I want to end with a note of caution. We must ensure that we are embarking upon songwriting for the primary reward of glorifying God – if we try to do it from any other motive we will end up disillusioned. We need to test our hearts, because we may be seeking to write songs so that we are recognised. If this is the case, we will be disappointed.

It is unlikely that you will find fame and fortune through worship songwriting. I have had five songs published and when I heard the first one would be in a songbook I joked with my wife that I would treat myself to a packet of crisps with the royalties. This was a gross overstatement of the financial rewards, as for the first four years I received nothing! I know from meeting a couple of leading Christian songwriters that their earnings from royalties are fairly modest, even though their songs are sung all over the world!

If you are looking for recognition, this, again, is likely to lead to disappointment. This is not meant to deter you from songwriting – just to encourage you to have a realistic view that many of your efforts may not be used at all, and others will experience limited use for a short period. However, if one of your songs helps your congregation to worship the Lord in a closer and more personal way, even for just one Sunday, that is a precious, and achievable, goal.

Ultimately our aim as songwriters is to give God glory and pleasure by glorifying his name. When I read David's psalms I believe that I can sense the Lord's pleasure in David's expressions of love, adoration and praise. When my children were small their artwork (which will never be hung in the National Gallery) still gave me, their father, great pleasure. I believe that songs that will never be played publicly can still bring our Father in heaven pleasure as we seek to express our devotion and love for him.

Points to remember

- *David's songs are memorable* because they had coherent themes and lyrics that everyone could identify with. They expressed truth about God's character and what he has done. They came from real experience, and from the 'secret place' of David's relationship with God.

- *David's songs had form.* They were the result of songwriting craftsmanship. We need to use skill to work on original ideas, particularly in the areas of:

  Lyrics, which must:
  - fit the tune
  - be consistent in length across the song
  - contain sound doctrine
  - blend sympathetically with the melody.

  Range and key, which should be suitable for a congregation.

  Hooks, which help our songs to be memorable.

  Simplicity. If a song will be used in congregational worship a large group of people will sing it and therefore it must be simple to learn.

- *Feedback on our songs.* We need to have a group of people we can ask to give us honest feedback about the quality of the songs we have written.

- *'Hit' ratio.* Some of David's songs were more memorable than others – we may have to write a lot of songs before we compose something that is really good. We must not be discouraged at a low 'hit' ratio.

Questions for personal application

1. Think about songs that especially help you to worship. What is good about them?

2. Think about songs that your congregation especially respond to in worship (not just your friends, but across age ranges). Again, what are the features of these songs? Are the features different from the songs you especially like?

3. If you've written songs try to rank them in order of quality. What makes the top three better than those lower down your list?

4. Analyse some new worship songs using the song assessment sheet in Appendix III.

5. If you wrote a song who would be the honest critics you would ask for feedback?

CHAPTER 8

David: The prophetic worshipper

> Brothers, I can tell you confidently that the patriarch David died and was buried, and his tomb is here to this day. But he was a prophet and knew that God had promised him on oath that he would place one of his descendants on his throne.
>
> *Acts 2:29-30*

David was clearly a man with prophetic gifting. As we will see, he prophesied Christ's death and resurrection roughly one thousand years before Jesus' birth.

Peter, speaking to the crowd at Pentecost in Acts 2, quotes extensively from two of David's psalms in his powerful sermon to the crowd to demonstrate that Jesus is the Christ. Psalm 16, quoted in Acts 2:25-28, refers to Jesus' resurrection. The Holy One is not David, who 'died and was buried', but the Christ who was not abandoned to the grave but raised to life. Psalm 110 (quoted in Acts 2:34-35) relates to the exalted, ascended Messiah.

Another example of prophetic gift in David's psalms is Psalm 22, in which David predicts the Messiah's agony on the cross.

We can be prophetic, too

When we read passages of this power we can think that prophetic gifting is purely for biblical superstars such as David and not for ordinary believers. In fact, the New Testament makes it clear that God has revealed his will and his wisdom to each one of us. 1 Corinthians 2:11-15 illustrates this point:

> The Spirit searches all things, even the deep things of God. For who among men knows the thoughts of a man except the man's spirit within him? In the same way no one knows the thoughts of God except the Spirit of God. We have not received the spirit of the world but the Spirit who is from God, that we may understand what God has freely given us . . . 'For who has known the mind of the Lord that he may instruct him?' But we have the mind of Christ.

The phrase 'we have the mind of Christ' is astonishing. Though we were dead in our transgressions and sins God has made us alive in Christ and given us his Spirit. Though we are 'jars of clay', we have God's treasure within us. We have received God's Spirit into our lives.

Having the mind of Christ does not mean that every idea that enters our heads is from the Lord! 1 Corinthians 13:9 makes it clear that 'we know in part and we prophesy in part', and our human fallibility is all too evident. Sometimes we will make mistakes and should be very open to this possibility. However, some Christians do not believe that God can speak through them at all. Yet if David, in an age before the Holy Spirit was poured out at Pentecost, had such great anointing, then surely we, whom the Bible describes as 'children of God' (1 John 3:1), can also receive wisdom and insight from the Lord.

In worship we are focusing our minds, and indeed our whole beings, toward God. We should expect that this is a time (although certainly not the only time) when we will receive prophetic insight from him.

How do we define 'prophetic'?

Before we look at prophetic worship more fully, perhaps we should try to explain what we mean by 'prophetic'. There is a very helpful definition in Wayne Grudem's *Systematic Theology:**

> . . . it should be defined not as 'predicting the future', nor as 'proclaiming a word from the Lord' nor as 'powerful preaching', but rather as 'telling something that God has spontaneously brought to mind'.

Sometimes we can find the concept of prophecy intimidating because we believe that it must be the foretelling of some great and mighty event in the future. However, if we expand our definition to 'telling something that God has spontaneously brought to mind', prophecy instantly appears more accessible.

We can see how God brings something spontaneously to David's mind, which he 'tells' and it has a lasting impact. This would not just apply to Psalms 16 and 110, mentioned above, but also to a psalm such as Psalm 23. As David considers the shepherd's care of the sheep he senses that God is speaking to him of the Father's love for his people. An everyday activity now resonates with supernatural power.

The prophetic is about a relationship

It is important to emphasise that the prophetic comes out of a relationship with our Lord. The more time we spend with him the more we will know him and what his thoughts and feelings are. My wife knows me very well and therefore in many situations she knows how I am feeling. There will be times when I will tell her my thoughts directly, at others she can tell, just from my body language, how I am, even though others in the same room would not know. The more we deepen our relationship with the Lord the more we will be able to develop prophetically.

---

* InterVarsity Press, 1994, p1049.

Furthermore, just as my wife understands my feelings through my explicit communication or through more subtle indications, there will times when you will be clear that God has spoken to you, and others when you have only a faint inclination of what the Lord wants to say. Understanding whether the prompting you experience is really from the Lord takes time, experience and lots of mistakes! I have been bringing prophetic contributions in meetings for more than twenty years and know I still have an enormous amount to learn. But unless we take some risks by speaking out what we believe God is saying we will never know whether we are right or not!

If we wish to develop our relationship with the Lord so that we have greater discernment over what his thoughts and feelings are it is essential that we get to know his word, the Bible. I am interested in Winston Churchill: I have therefore read books about him and also books written by him. This has helped me to understand far more about his character and attitudes. If we wish to deepen our understanding of God's character we must immerse ourselves in his teachings and the accounts of the things that he does that are given to us in the Bible.

Furthermore, it is essential that every prophetic contribution must be in line with God's revelation of himself in Scripture. The Lord does not act in a manner that is inconsistent with Scripture. 'I the Lord do not change' (Malachi 3:6). 'Jesus Christ is the same yesterday and today and for ever' (Hebrews 13:8). If the 'prophetic' message that goes through our minds is inconsistent with the Bible it is not from God!

When I think I may have a prophetic contribution I compare it with my knowledge of the Scriptures, trying to find if there is a biblical precedent for what I think God may be saying. If I can't think of one then I will abandon the idea! If I can think of one then I may mention this when I bring the prophetic word, or read a suitable verse as I believe that linking what I say with Scripture gives what I will say greater weight.

What is prophetic worship?

Based on Grudem's definition we could describe this as 'the musical and lyrical expression of something that God has spontaneously brought to mind'.

The most memorable worship times I have been in are those where this has happened. God has spoken to someone in the congregation. They have expressed it, the musicians have provided an appropriate musical accompaniment, and the meeting has suddenly become infused with a fresh and powerful dynamic, where we are certain we are worshipping in spirit and truth.

Let me provide you with some examples from my own experience. One worship time I was leading some years ago had not been going well! However, someone from the congregation came out to the front of the meeting and started singing from Psalm 23, about how God's love 'will follow me *all* the days of my life, not just some of the days, but *all* of the days'. This improvised song suddenly seemed the most appropriate expression of what God was saying to us. God had spontaneously brought something to mind, she had 'told it' in song, and suddenly the meeting was transformed from being dull and uninspiring to being full of the presence of God. The musicians contributed greatly by adapting their style of playing: the electric guitarist started playing reggae, the rest of the band followed suit and suddenly the musical environment had changed, and perfectly followed the tone of the song being sung.

At another meeting someone came up to the front and said – 'I think we should sing the name "Jesus" over and over.' As worship leader I had to immediately compose a tune and chord sequence, which was challenging, but the musicians and the congregation took it up and it was a powerful time. Again God had spontaneously brought something to mind and congregation and musicians all responded together.

It is hard to describe the change in atmosphere. I would liken it to visiting the 'Rapids' swimming pool at Center Parcs. At some points you have to wade, working hard to get through the water, and then suddenly you find yourself being pushed along at an exhilarating pace! Sometimes during worship it feels as if we have suddenly found ourselves in God's 'rapids': it was heavy going then suddenly we were drawn into a new awareness of God's presence.

In our church there is a great deal of spontaneous contribution but this level of anointing does not happen every week. However, I believe that God's will for his church is for us to experience more anointed, prophetic contributions such as these, that are accompanied by sensitive musicians, also inspired by the Holy Spirit. When this happens all the people – musicians and congregation – join together, flow together and experience a new level of awareness of the presence of God.

How can we facilitate prophetic worship in our churches?

- Create an environment in your church where contributions, especially prophecy, are encouraged.
- Pray for anointed contributions.
- In preparation for leading worship pray for a theme that in itself is prophetic.
- Be prophetic musically.

It is this last point that we will look at further.

How can we be prophetic musically?

The Old Testament in general, and David's time in particular, refers to musicians playing in ways that minister to people.

Musical pauses ('Selah') help the congregation to meditate on the Lord

As musicians we can provide an appropriate accompaniment

to assist the congregation in their reflection upon the Lord. We should not be afraid of musical interludes: the psalms are full of such pauses. David Fellingham puts it like this:

> Sometimes in the psalm there would be a 'Selah'. Thirty-nine of the psalms have the word 'Selah', twenty-eight of which give musical descriptions in their inscription. Although there is some vagueness about the exact meaning of the word, there is strong evidence to suggest that it was a musical interlude. The musicians would pick up the mood of what had been expressed and illustrate it musically. This would then give the congregation opportunity to meditate on the words and ask God for understanding. Music is a very powerful means of communication and Selahs, when they are played skilfully by anointed musicians, can help a congregation to respond in their hearts to God. The use of the word 'Selah' in the Psalms suggests that the music played expressed different moods. So the Selah in Psalm 55, where the psalmist is expressing his desire for escape and to find refuge, would have very different musical content from the triumphant note of the Selah in Psalm 49.*

When I am not in the band but am in the congregation I find such 'Selahs' or musical interludes very helpful to reflect and meditate on the Lord. I do not find it conducive to worship if we sing several songs, one after another, with no opportunity to pause or reflect.

Music can minister the grace of God to people – particularly troubled individuals

> Whenever the spirit from God came upon Saul, David would take his harp and play. Then relief would come to Saul; he would feel better, and the evil spirit would leave him.
>
> *1 Samuel 16:23*

---

* David Fellingham, *Worship Restored*, Kingsway, 1987, p. 47.

When David played to Saul he clearly ministered God's grace and peace to him. I have sometimes seen musicians bless an individual in this way by playing near them. It doesn't mean they were oppressed by an evil spirit! It is one way in which we as musicians can communicate God's love and grace to a person.

I believe that we can apply this in a wider context: when you play in a worship time have faith that you are not just providing an accompaniment for the singing but are actively communicating God's love and grace to the congregation in the music that you play.

As musicians we should be in faith that, though flawed ourselves, we do have the 'mind of Christ', which means that we will be able to communicate something of God's love for people through our playing. I have found it helpful to remind myself of this and to seek to actively 'tune in' to God when playing electric guitar in worship. If there is a 'Selah' I will sometimes sing words of worship in English or in tongues and try to play what I am singing.

Prophesying with instruments

> David . . . set apart some of the sons of Asaph, Heman and Jeduthun for the ministry of prophesying, accompanied by harps, lyres and cymbals. Here is the list of the men who performed this service . . . who prophesied, using the harp in thanking and praising the Lord.
>
> *1 Chronicles 25:1-3*

The first reference to prophecy appears to imply that those set apart spoke or sang prophecy, accompanied by their instruments. Verse 3 is more ambiguous – does this mean that the 'prophecies' were instrumentals, with no words?

There is no doubt that music can provide an appropriate accompaniment to sung prophecy. It is essential that the musicians are sensitive. First of all they must not drown out the singer, as the words must be heard by the congregation; neither must they intrude or distract the congregation from the message itself. However, as musicians become more confident they can modify their playing to reflect the tone of the message, for example playing gently for fatherly words of encouragement, or more forcefully for proclamations of God's power.

I have not experienced many instances where musicians have played instrumentals without voices in a way that might be described as prophesying. I did hear of one meeting several years ago where, after the congregation had prayed together regarding terrible events that had occurred in a particular country, an anointed and skilful trumpeter played a solo which, to many in the meeting, expressed God's sadness over the situation.

Music can inspire the prophetic

2 Kings 3:11-20 gives an illustration of how prophecy comes after a musician plays. Elisha requests a musician to play to inspire him prophetically, and 'While the harpist was playing, the hand of the Lord came upon Elisha.'

Music can help create an atmosphere. Most restaurants and bars use music to help to set the tone of their establishment, whether it's gentle classical, jazz or dance music. As Christian musicians we contribute to an environment which helps our congregations focus on the Lord and therefore encourages the prophetic. However, I am not talking about 'wallpaper' music, a passive background sound, but music in which both musicians and congregation are actively seeking the Lord. It may be appropriate in certain meetings to allow the musicians to play for a few moments in the expectation that someone in the congregation will receive a word from the Lord.

Worship has an impact upon the enemy

In 2 Chronicles 20:22 Jehoshaphat appoints singers to worship the Lord at the front of the army. 'As they began to sing and praise, the Lord set ambushes against the men of Ammon and Moab and Mount Seir who were invading Judah, and they were defeated.' I do not know exactly how this happened, but what is clear is that when we worship the Lord something occurs in the heavenly places that affects us here on earth. Psalm 8:2 says that the Lord has ordained praise from the lips of children and infants 'because of your enemies, to silence the foe and the avenger'. Worship is a powerful weapon against the enemy. In the words of Wesley Duewel in his book *Touch the World through Prayer,** 'Praise pierces the darkness, dynamites long-standing obstructions and sends the demons of hell fleeing.'

'Taking up' a song

In Exodus 15, after the Lord has miraculously delivered the Israelites from the Egyptian army, it says that Moses and the Israelites sang a song to the Lord. The song must have been spontaneous as no one could have predicted beforehand what God would do! Yet it says that it was not just Moses who sang but the people as well. I can't be definitive about what happened, but my guess is that Moses began singing the song and then everyone else joined in, thus declaring God's majesty and power together.

Sometimes when someone in our church brings a prophetic song there will be a particular phrase that stands out as being particularly significant. At the end of the song I will then get the congregation to sing this phrase. To join in with the song helps us to respond actively to what God is saying, and the repetition helps us to get hold of the message and to declare it ourselves (although we must be careful not to

---

* Zondervan (Grand Rapids Michigan USA), 1986.

repeat it so much it loses its impact!). I may also vary the song by getting the congregation to sing different words to the same tune that also reflect the message that has been brought.

Another way you can lead people to sing a prophetic song is to sing a line and get the congregation to repeat it.

All of this means you have to 'think on your feet' and really tests your inventiveness! There have been several times when I have got the congregation to sing with me, changing lines every few times and then I have found that I've run out of ideas! I then swiftly draw the song to a conclusion, or encourage the congregation to sing in the Spirit. I have fallen flat on my face a few times, but when it works it is a great way of engaging everyone in a musical response to God's prophetic word to his people.

How do we grow in prophetic worship?

Believe we have the mind of Christ

First of all we should take God at his word and believe that we do hear from him. Believe that he will inspire you, in words and songs, and also in musical accompaniment.

Desire spiritual gifts

1 Corinthians 14:1 says, 'eagerly desire spiritual gifts, especially the gift of prophecy.' Verse 39 urges us to 'be eager to prophesy'. The Bible commands us to desire spiritual gifts for ourselves as individuals, and for our church. Pray specifically for spiritual gifts, both for yourself and for others in your church.

Make room for the Holy Spirit

Who transforms worship times from singing a few songs to powerful times in which we encounter God? It is the Holy Spirit, through his empowerment and gifts. Let us welcome him, and make room for him in our worship times. If we sing one song after another throughout the worship we leave no space for the spontaneous. As worship leaders we must leave 'pauses' in worship so that people can participate. If we leave no room we will not receive any contributions.

Take risks

We cannot experience prophetic worship without taking some risks. Expressing musically something that God has spontaneously brought to mind cannot be rehearsed (although it can be practised – see later). Therefore, whether we are the individual who brings the prophetic contribution or the musicians who provide accompaniment we have to be spontaneous. This means that we will probably get it wrong some of the time. The fear that we may get it wrong may paralyse us from attempting something, even though our idea is right.

Be encouraged and take risks! It is helpful, if you are in leadership, to give people permission to attempt things and for them to know that you will support them for their courage and initiative, even if they get things wrong.

Practice

There is a saying that 'spontaneous brilliance requires earlier diligence'. While we cannot rehearse the spontaneous, we can practise so that we feel to some degree prepared for it. You may find it helpful to play your instrument on your own, seeking to convey a particular emotion. Perhaps turn to a psalm and try to communicate the psalmist's feelings musically. If you play piano or guitar, try singing a psalm over your own spontaneous backing. These times on your own will help you when the Lord prompts you to start playing or singing in a meeting.

Similarly at band rehearsals you can play spontaneously together. Choose a psalm and get one of your vocalists to sing it, while the band improvises a musical backing. The following points may help:

- *Ask God to lead you as you play*

  Pray that God will help you to express something of his character in your playing – his love, splendour, majesty, compassion – whatever is the appropriate aspect at the time. Sing in tongues and try to play what you're singing. Meditate on the Lord and try to express how you feel towards him.

- *Take risks*

  A rehearsal is a private place in which you can make mistakes. Attempt things that are outside your comfort zone. It really doesn't matter if you mess things up! Only a few people can hear!

- *Listen to each other*

  While it is good for everyone to have free expression in their playing, there must also be a sense of order. If every-one plays a solo at the same time it will be chaotic, which is not biblical! 1 Corinthians 14:33 says, 'For God is not a God of disorder but of peace.' Ephesians 5:21, in the context of worship, says 'Submit to one another out of reverence for Christ.' Your band will need to defer to one another. While one plays simple accompaniment another can attempt to express the appropriate emotion in a solo. It is often helpful for some of the band to take a break from playing, then come in later, perhaps as others cease playing for a few moments. This gives a sense of variety and prevents the sound from becoming too cluttered. We must also listen carefully to each other to pick up the nuances of each other's playing. The most competent musicians I have worked with have one common characteristic – they are great listeners. They identify what others play and fit their own parts round them. In the example I gave of the guitarist playing reggae, what one person played changed the whole mood and style of the musical accompaniment. The others in the band aligned their style with the appropriate backing that one musician had initiated.

Pitfalls and safeguards

While I encourage you wholeheartedly to step out and take risks with the aim of being prophetic musicians, there are some pitfalls.

1. We prophesy in part

As I mentioned before, having the mind of Christ does not mean that every idea that enters our heads is from the Lord! Furthermore, sometimes we will hear from God but we speak at the wrong time during the worship. For more guidance on this please see Appendix I on leading worship. If we are in tune with the Holy Spirit we will find that he has given gifts to others in the congregation along the same theme. This helps to encourage them and us that we have heard correctly.

2. Take the congregation with you

There is a danger that in seeking to initiate prophetic worship we musicians can end up playing in a way that exhilarates us but loses the rest of the congregation. It is very important that we continue to serve the congregation. Mindful of this, I have found that in many meetings it is not appropriate to launch out in this manner. I pray and wait for the appropriate moment when we can seize the opportunity, having practised as a band on our own. When we step out in this way it is helpful to say a few words of explanation to the congregation so that they know what we are trying to do.

3. Be submissive

All aspects of worship are under the authority of your church leadership. It is essential that they are happy with any intended change to the style or content of church worship. It is often helpful to discuss the direction you would like to go in with your leaders, and if some unusual development occurs in a meeting talk it through with them, both specifically and generally. Ultimately what pleases the Lord is a submissive and willing spirit who respects spiritual authority.

4. Be discipled

Ask friends, including church leaders, 'How could I have improved that?' Seek continually to improve the way that you serve your church in your own prophetic contributions and the musical accompaniment you provide. 'He who ignores discipline despises himself, but whoever heeds correction gains understanding' (Proverbs 15:32).

Prophetic worship is an exciting adventure as we discover what God has for us. Let's press on, with excitement in our hearts, to experience more of what David knew – and more!

Points to remember

- *David had amazing prophetic gifting* – but as New Testament believers we too can receive spiritual gifts.

- *Prophecy is not necessarily 'predicting the future'* but rather 'telling something that God has spontaneously brought to mind'.

- *The prophetic is about a relationship with the Lord.* The more we know him we the more we know his thoughts and feelings – but this can never contradict God's revelation of himself in Scripture.

- *We can be prophetic musically* through:
  - musical interludes ('Selahs') to help the congregation meditate on the Lord

- ministering the grace of God to individuals and to the congregation
- prophesying accompanied by and with instruments
- responding musically to prophetic song.

- *Beware of pitfalls:*
  - Remember that we prophesy in part and will make mistakes.
  - Take the congregation with you.
  - Be submissive to your leadership.
  - Be discipled.

Questions for application

1. Can you think of situations where you have experienced prophetic worship? How would you describe it?

2. Have there been occasions on which you have felt prompted to play or sing something spontaneous in a church meeting but did not proceed? What stopped you? On reflection, would it have been right to initiate what you had in mind?

3. How can you work with other musicians to 'practise' spontaneity?

CHAPTER 9

David and Bathsheba: Falling into grace (2 Samuel 11)

We cannot read the story of David and Bathsheba without being shocked. How can a man who walks so closely with God be guilty not just of adultery but of an appalling cover-up, and ultimately of murder?

David is clearly a role model for musicians and worship leaders in many respects, but not in this one! However, as we read through the story we can still find many areas that can speak to us, both in helping us understand our vulnerability to temptation and, if we fall, how our relationship with God can be restored.

Sadly, David's story is not the only one of a musician becoming involved in sexual immorality. I have been aware of several instances where this has occurred. They have all, without exception, been people whom I would never have expected to have problems of this kind. All of us are vulnerable.

While this chapter concentrates on the area of sexual immortality, it is not the only temptation musicians may face. David received adulation: the women sang that he had 'slain his tens of thousands' (1 Samuel 18:7). Worship leaders, as well as military heroes, can be the subject of admiration and we can find the idea of being a worship celebrity highly seductive! If we are in charge of our group we may find we are tempted to dominate and control. We need to be wary of every trap we could fall into.

Falling into grace

The phrase 'fall from grace' is often used, for instance when a politician is discovered to have behaved badly in some way and has to leave office. A wonderful aspect of David's story is that, for all the terrible tragedy of the adultery, deception and murder that he indulged in, David falls *into* grace – he receives mercy and forgiveness from the Lord. I believe that David learns more about God's character through this terrible experience than before.

So – how does someone who appears to be so close to God fall? We shall never know exactly why but the story does contain some indications.

David was in a place of ease

After so many years of struggle, David's position as king was secure. The Israelite army was successful – even without David at its command it destroyed the Ammonites (verse 1). In the past, David had experienced difficulties and it is clear that during these years he was dependent upon God. In Psalm 59, concerning his escape from Saul's palace, he writes: 'O my Strength, I watch for you; you, O God, are my fortress, my loving God' (verse 9). When he hides from Saul in the cave he writes: 'Have mercy on me, O God, have mercy on me, for in you my soul takes refuge' (Psalm 57:1).

When we are in a place of peril, needing God's intervention in our lives, we depend upon him and cling closely to him. But in 2 Samuel 11 David is no longer conscious of his need for God – and is therefore in far greater danger than at the hands of Saul or the Philistines! Matthew Henry writes of 1 Samuel 11, 'let him that readeth understand what the best of men are, when God leaves them to themselves.'*

---

* Matthew Henry, *A Commentary on the Holy Bible*, Marshall Brothers, Limited, 1961, p. 803.

The chapter commences by stating that the spring is a time when kings go to war, but instead of utilising his military genius for the good of God's people, we find that David has delegated responsibility to Joab. The instructions Joab gives the messenger in verses 19 to 21 show that Joab perceived that David had lost none of his sharpness for the detail of battle, or for the need to constantly learn from the past (e.g. the woman throwing the millstone at Thebez in verse 21). David was a man made for battle: when he opts out he gets himself into problems. Surely the battleground was a place where David's dependence upon the Lord would have been renewed.

There is one battle we can never opt out of. The devil is seeking to defeat us – constantly! 1 Peter 5:8 says that 'Your enemy the devil prowls around like a roaring lion looking for someone to devour.' You cannot agree a cessation of hostilities with the enemy while you take a rest!

Worship is a key area of church life. The story of Jehoshaphat in 2 Chronicles 20:20-30 shows that worship has an impact upon the spiritual battle we are waging. If the enemy can damage an area of the church that has a major influence on the spiritual war, you can be sure he will target it. Furthermore, worship is a sensitive area – God's people are directly communicating with him, corporately. As we seek to engage with him with all our hearts and minds, any impurity in the church will have a negative impact upon our worship.

The enemy can inflict a great deal of damage on the church when he is able to pull down public figures. You may not realise it, but as a worship leader or a musician you hold a prominent position in the church. If you fall, this will cause great heartache to the people in your church because of the trust they place in their leaders. If any scandal becomes public this damages our churches even further.

It is a strange oxymoron that when we are most conscious of our weakness we are actually safest as we put our trust in

God. When we think we are standing we need to take care lest we fall! (see 1 Corinthians 10:12).

I have always found the external disciplines of having to lead meetings, be they small groups or larger meetings, very helpful for my spiritual life. The responsibility of leading forces me to be dependent on God. On the other hand, holidays and periods like Christmas can be times when it's very easy to switch off from the spiritual life and lose ground. It is therefore good to be aware of our vulnerability over these relaxing periods.

There have been other times when I have had to trust God simply to get through the day. One agonising period at work springs to mind! While this was in many ways unpleasant, I treasure the closeness with God that developed during that season. I don't think that it's scriptural to wish testing or hardship upon ourselves, but God does use these phases of our lives to encourage us to depend on him. Unfortunately, sometimes when we move from a season of trials into a season of blessing, we can lose our focus on the Lord.

David was vulnerable

David's vulnerability was not on the battlefield. It was when he was relaxing in his palace. When are you vulnerable? Is it at the office party? Is it when you're on the internet at home? We need to understand when we ourselves are vulnerable to temptation. While the story of David and Bathsheba concerns sexual sin, each of us is tempted in many different ways.

We do not know if this was the first time David had walked around on the roof and just happened to see Bathsheba. Or it may be that he was in the habit of peering from the roof into private gardens. Sin can occur as a 'one-off', or may arise after habitually putting oneself in danger. Either way we must consider our vulnerabilities and take drastic action. Jesus said that if our right eye causes us to sin we must gouge it out! (Matthew 5:29). I do not believe that he meant literal self-mutilation, but rather a radical approach to lifestyle so that we do not place ourselves in temptation.

David did not have accountable friendships

In his teenage years David was blessed with the friendship of Jonathan, Saul's son. They were very close, with Jonathan becoming 'one in spirit with David' (1 Samuel 18:1). Jonathan showed altruistic love to David, giving him his tunic, sword, bow and belt and putting his own life in danger for his friend.

After Jonathan dies in battle, there is little further evidence of close friendship in David's life. We read in 1 Chronicles 27:33 that 'Hushai the Arkite was the king's friend', so clearly David was not friendless, but there is no evidence of the same level of closeness as with Jonathan. It is possible for us to have a wide circle of friends, without anyone really knowing us well.

Consequently there is no close friend to warn David that he should be going into battle rather than resting. Later, a friend would have noticed David acting suspiciously in trying to get Uriah to come to the palace and might have challenged David as to what was going on! A friend could have said a few words that might have averted sin entirely or stopped David from compounding his error.

Nathan the prophet is there to speak God's word to David; however, this is as an authority figure once things have gone horribly wrong. We can be sure that our church leaders will bring godly correction to us if we have fallen, but we may not have sufficiently close relationships with them that they will spot the warning signs and detect that something is going wrong in our lives at an early stage. It is important to have a few friends who can ask us tough questions such as the real state of our marriages and the quality of our spiritual lives. We need to be honest and open with them and receive their prayers and counsel when things are not going as well as they should. Friendship is important for many reasons, and one of these is that it safeguards us from sin.

David thought he was above the law

David had a clear sense of godly justice – we see how he burns with anger at the iniquity of the situation Nathan describes in 2 Samuel 12. He would have been conscious of the law, which states that adultery was punishable by death (Leviticus 20:10). So why does he do something so wrong himself?

There are probably many answers to this, but one reason may be that with all his power and gifting he somehow feels superior to everyone else – that he could do things that others were not permitted to.

Power and position can, if we are not careful, corrupt us. They give us opportunity to do things that others could not achieve. A church treasurer will have opportunity to embezzle funds in a way far beyond the average church member!

David was loved by women. The women (not the men) sang that David had 'slain his tens of thousands' – his popularity and position, as well as his handsome appearance (1 Samuel 16:12) gave him opportunities with women that no one else in Israel would have. Besides, who would challenge the king?

We may find it strange, but our position in church life as musicians and worship leaders can make us the object of respect and affection. This can give us a heady sense of power. We must be careful not to abuse our authority within church life – whether it's with church finances or, as in David's case, in the area of sexual conduct.

In 2 Samuel 12 David displayed clear views regarding the morality of the situation Nathan describes, but he does not apply the same standards to himself. If we ever do anything that we would counsel others against doing, then we are in grave danger. We must be stringent with our conduct. Remember that anyone who is a teacher incurs a stricter judgement (James 3:1).

Emotional attachment through music

Music is one of God's greatest gifts to mankind. It expresses emotions more powerfully than words. It can change our mood, making us feel like dancing or crying. Creating music can be an almost transcendent experience, and when we work in teams to produce music together we 'bond' with each other. In practising for a particular event all those involved will feel the tension of preparing, and the exhilaration upon successful completion of the concert/worship time. This is a powerful experience that can be very positive in bringing a strong sense of fellowship to your band. We should, however, be careful if we are working closely with someone of the opposite sex.

Making music is time consuming. We can spend many hours with other musicians. It may not just be a case of playing together, but also of travelling, eating and generally socialising together. Such fellowship is a great blessing, but it is unwise to spend large amounts of time on your own with a band member of the opposite sex.

As the husband of a wife who is not involved in church music I need to be conscious that she can feel left out as she is not attending the rehearsals or participating in many of the events I am involved in. Men can sometimes find it difficult to communicate thoughts and feelings and I sometimes have to make a conscious effort to express my emotions over current music projects, partly so that she feels involved, but also because I can then benefit from her wisdom and perspective. We must ensure that we cleave to our spouses and do not allow music to pull us away from them.

Getting away with it?

Up until the end of chapter 11 we might think that David has got away with it. He has successfully covered up the scandal – Uriah has been killed in battle and Bathsheba has now attained the respectable status of the king's wife. We can think with sin that we can get away with it, that it is unseen. This may be true with regard to the eyes of men, but the last verse leaves us in no doubt as to the spiritual reality: 'But the thing David had done displeased the Lord.' God is the eternal witness of all our thoughts, words and deeds and, sure enough, David is brought to account. David falls – but he falls into the wonderful, forgiving grace of God.

Confessing sin

David's conduct is far from God's standards, but his conscience remains sufficiently sensitive that when Nathan confronts him he immediately admits 'I have sinned against the Lord' (2 Samuel 12:13). While David has undoubtedly harmed Uriah specifically and the kingdom of Israel as a whole, he acknowledges that ultimately it is God he has disobeyed and God to whom he must give an account.

There is great power in confession, in admitting that we have done wrong, and in being willing to change our ways. Psalm 32, which some commentators believe was composed following David's adultery with Bathsheba, states:

> When I kept silent, my bones wasted away through my
>   groaning all day long. For day and night your hand
>   was heavy upon me;
> my strength was sapped as in the heat of summer.
> Then I acknowledged my sin to you
> and did not cover up my iniquity.
> I said, 'I will confess my transgression to the Lord' –
> and you forgave the guilt of my sin.

While we are unrepentant we are in a state that is mentally and physical debilitating. Our rebellion against God means that we have closed ourselves off from his peace and we have effectively given sin free reign in our lives. The Holy Spirit is bringing pressure on us to turn away from our wrongdoing.

We may be difficult people to be around in this condition, because our hardness of heart and denial of guilt may make us irritable. When we confess our sin it is as if we have opened a door once again to the grace and mercy of God, and we can see from Psalm 32 the instant impact this has upon David.

Through his repentance, David experiences new revelation about the Lord. I am sure that he has always known that God is not pleased with sacrifices that were not accompanied by contrition, but now, in Psalm 51, he expresses this fully: 'You do not delight in sacrifice, or I would bring it . . . The sacrifices of God are a broken spirit; a broken and contrite heart, O God, you will not despise.'

Total forgiveness and restoration

Psalm 51, the title of which states that it was written by David after Nathan had confronted him, is not just a psalm of repentance, but also a clear declaration that there is full restoration for the repentant sinner. The tone is not of a man begging for forgiveness but of someone who knows that his Lord is full of grace and mercy and wishes to restore him. After confessing his sin David asks the Lord to 'cleanse' him so that he is 'whiter than snow' (verse 7) and to 'blot out' his 'iniquity' (verse 9). These are amazing requests – that a man who is an adulterer, a liar and murderer could ever be perceived in the eyes of God as 'whiter than snow'. Yet this is the truth of the gospel. 'If we confess our sins, he is faithful and just and will forgive us our sins and purify us from all unrighteousness' (1 John 1:9). Not only this but God chooses not to remember our transgressions: 'Their sins and lawless acts I will remember no more' (Hebrews 10:17).

But David goes even beyond this. He asks the Lord not just to forgive him, but to change him: 'Create in me a pure heart, O God, and renew a steadfast spirit within me . . . Restore to me the joy of your salvation and grant me a willing spirit, to sustain me' (Psalm 51:10-12). He clearly knows that the Lord does not just want to 'blot out' sin, but also to change the sinner so that he becomes, once again, a willing servant of the Lord, to restore him to the intimate relationship he once had with his Creator.

While David must bear some consequences because of his sin, his relationship with God is totally restored. If you have sinned in any area of your life, I urge you strongly to confess it both to God and to others. You will face consequences, but nothing is more important than the restoration of your relationship with God.

Disqualified?

David knew that the Lord could not only forgive him, but restore him to his former ministry. In Psalm 51, after asking the Lord to change him, he says, 'then I will teach transgressors your ways . . . O Lord, open my lips, and my mouth will declare your praise' (verses 13-15). The sinner can be restored once again to become a teacher and a worshipper.

If you have fallen you may feel permanently disqualified. One man I spoke with said that he could never forget that he committed adultery many years ago and felt he was therefore permanently barred from any form of church leadership whatsoever.

If we have sinned in a way that damages our relationships and our church then there will inevitably be a period during which we have to restore the trust of those around us. It will probably be inappropriate for us to have leadership responsibility during this time. However, to consider ourselves to be permanently disbarred is too extreme an approach in my view. David still had a massive contribution to make to the people of God and his restoration itself speaks to us. We will still be able to serve the Lord in our generation – just as David did.

Guard your heart!

Proverbs 4:23 tells us, 'Above all else, guard your heart, for it is the wellspring of life.' We are vulnerable beings who are easily seduced by what the world has to offer. Jesus taught his disciples how to pray – and this included 'lead us not into temptation, but deliver us from the evil one' (Matthew 6:13). To prevent our weak and foolish hearts from going astray we must continue to focus our lives upon the Lord and also pray that he will keep us safe.

Points to remember

- *David fell when he was in a place of ease.* We may be more vulnerable when things are going well than when we are having to depend upon God.
- *David did not have accountable friendships.* We need to have friends who know us well and who will challenge us if they believe that we are going off track.
- *Making music together 'bonds' us with others.* While this is precious we must be wary of forming inappropriate emotional attachments with those of the opposite sex.
- *If we confess our sin God will forgive us and restore us.*
- *Scripture commands us to guard our hearts.* The world, the flesh and the devil are seeking to seduce us from following the Lord.

Questions for personal application

1. What are the areas in your life where you are most vulnerable to temptation?
2. When do you feel most vulnerable in these areas? What action can you take to protect yourself?
3. Do you have a 'Jonathan' – a close friend who knows where you are vulnerable and will challenge you in these areas?

CHAPTER 10

Succession (2 Samuel 7)

David was one of the Bible's most gifted individuals. God clearly anointed him as a leader, musician and songwriter. Multi-talented though he was, even he had to face the fact that his ministry was temporary and that God did not intend him to accomplish every task he desired. The building of a temple for the Lord, which David longed for, was achieved by someone else.

If these principles are true for David, how much more so for us! It is tempting for us to believe that the roles and responsibilities God gives to us are permanent, when in fact they are only for a season. Sometimes others will accomplish the visions and dreams we have, and not ourselves.

It is important that, like David, we respond positively to these challenges:

David's desire is godly (2 Samuel 7:2)

David's desire to build a temple of the Lord clearly comes from godly motives. While God's purpose is that someone else will fulfil that vision, he does not criticise David for holding that desire. In fact, the Lord commends him – in 1 Kings 8:17 Solomon says: 'My father David had it in his heart to build a temple for the Name of the Lord, the God of Israel. But the Lord said to my father David, "Because it was in your heart to build a temple for my Name, you did well to have this in your heart."'

If someone else implements the vision we had, we may feel that we were inadequate for the task. In fact, God says that we do well to have the desire in our hearts.

Clarity of vision comes through expression

It is interesting to speculate what might have happened (or not happened) if David had chosen not to articulate his feelings in verse 2. Perhaps there would have been no prophecy from Nathan, and David would not have received the clear direction that comes in this chapter.

We can be tempted not to share our spiritual desires and ambitions with anyone. We can be fearful lest others believe our ideas are born out of selfish ambition, or are unworkable. We may even fear ridicule! Yet the lesson of this passage is that it is valuable to express our dreams to others, even if they are not fully developed. David did not have a detailed plan; he was just articulating a longing in his heart. Out of this situation comes very clear direction from the Lord, who provides far more than a 'yes' or 'no' response to David's desires.

The Lord's answer first of all clarifies David's theology. He reminds David that the history of his presence among his people has been on the basis of mobility. The ark, which David himself has restored to be among the people of Israel, is portable and God has never asked for a temple. While Solomon will be asked to build a house for the Lord, this in itself is temporary in purely physical terms, to be superseded by the 'spiritual house' made of 'living stones' of the New Covenant referred to in 1 Peter 2:5.

The Lord speaks of his protection of David: 'I have been with you wherever you have gone, and I have cut off all your enemies from before you' (verse 9), and then makes a number of promises regarding David's descendants. David had been looking to build a house for the Lord, but instead 'The Lord declares to you that the Lord himself will establish a house for you.' In the words of Michael Wilcox* 'What God does for David takes precedence over anything David can do for God.' No matter how big our ambitions are for God, when we give ourselves to him he will always repay us in greater measure!

Expressing our desires and ambitions to other people means that the Lord can use them as a channel for his word and direction. God speaks to Nathan 'that night' – the guidance came very quickly after David had expressed it. God did not allow David or Nathan to follow the wrong path for long.

David's reign was temporal

God's vision is always so much greater than ours. While David was primarily thinking of the practical 'bricks and mortar', the Lord's ideas are eternal. The prophecy through Nathan referred not only to the temporary nature of David's personal reign and that David's offspring would succeed him, but also to an eternal dynasty: 'I will establish the throne of his kingdom for ever' (verse 13). David's own involvement is temporary, but the plan of the Lord, which David is a part of, is eternal.

The Bible is full of heroes and heroines who served God faithfully and wholeheartedly in their generations and are a wonderful example and challenge to us all. However, all of them died once their season had concluded, and were succeeded by others who honoured the Lord in their time. Only Jesus has an eternal ministry (Hebrews 5:6).

All of us recognise the truth of this when applied to others; however, it may be more difficult to fully appreciate it for ourselves! While we may acknowledge to others that we know we are only temporary stewards of the role God has given us, it can be difficult for us to be truly ready to relinquish the position we have.

---

* *New Bible Commentary*, InterVarsity Press, 1994, p. 397.

We may also wish that we could serve the church in many different areas of ministry and feel frustrated we only have a limited amount of energy and cannot be involved in all of these.

Was it difficult for David to accept his mortality and the fact that someone else would accomplish his vision? He could have been angry with Nathan for changing his response from initial encouragement to saying that David would not be the person to build the temple. Instead, David responds in a godly manner.

David's heart is for his family and for the people of God
(2 Samuel 7:18-29)

David is clearly delighted that God has established a reign that will last forever and that his family and the people of Israel will prosper.

It is easy in western culture to become obsessed with our own role, and seek God's blessing for ourselves as individuals. Yet David is pleased that the Lord's blessing is upon the *community* of God's people. In the area of worship we can seek blessing on our own ministries, yet just as David sought blessing for the people, our focus should be on our community – the church.

God's plan is for our 'offspring to succeed us'
(2 Samuel 7:12)

God's design is for one of David's sons, Solomon, to succeed him. In our churches it is probably rare that our natural sons and daughters will step into our roles. Instead, it is often God's plan for spiritual 'sons and daughters' to take our place. Just as we aim to be an example to our natural children and train them in the way they should go, it is right to disciple those within the church who are less experienced than ourselves, but who ultimately have the potential to succeed us.

As worship leaders and musicians it is important to seek to identify those in our churches who have the potential to develop and to plan how we can develop them, giving them practical experience of playing and/or leading in different settings.

Here are a few things I have learned about training worship leaders:

- ***Smaller settings help to gain experience***

  For those leading our Sunday morning meetings there are a variety of pressures – the size of the meeting, managing the band and setting up the PA. These are in addition to actually leading worship! At one stage we had Sunday evening meetings in addition to the mornings. These were attended by far fewer people, were in a smaller hall and we used only a couple of instruments rather than a full band. These meetings were a great opportunity for our musicians to become experienced in leading worship without the additional pressures of the larger setting.

- ***Give them more than one opportunity***

  It is good to give someone more than one chance. I have found that in the area of public ministry you may not be able to draw any firm conclusions from the first occasion a person leads. On the one hand, the person themselves will probably be nervous and they may not feel relaxed enough to show their true gifting. On the other hand, you may find that the congregation wish to support the person to such an extent that they make a particular effort to support them and are more responsive than usual (this is an endearing trait!). It is in later times that you will be able to evaluate more conclusively how gifted the individual is at leading. You will also be able to evaluate the person's consistency if you give them several opportunities in quick succession.

- *Allow them to have preferences, disciple them over principles*

  When others lead worship they may choose to sing songs that I do not use when I lead worship and they may employ musical arrangements that are very different to my own. I have to consider whether this is merely a matter of preference of song style, in which case I must give them the freedom to lead in their own fashion, or whether what they have done contradicts a principle of worship leading that I hold dear (e.g. the songs should have scriptural truth within them). If the former is true I will give them the freedom to lead in their own style, if it is the latter I will talk to them about the principle so that next time their song selection will be mindful of this point.

- *Allow them to make mistakes*

  I showed my inexperience many times in my early days of leading worship – and still make many mistakes now! When we ask people to do things we must expect that they may make mistakes for the first few times at least. We must factor their inexperience into our assessment of how they have done, rather than expect them to do it as well as those who have many years' experience.

- *Training*

  While there is much one can pick up by watching our example, we cannot expect everyone to learn everything by osmosis. We need to set aside time to talk through the facets of our roles so that they have the information they need.

David came into the limelight when he fought Goliath because no one else wanted to take that role. I have sometimes found that people have been thrust forward because of particular circumstances. There have been several musicians who would not necessarily have had opportunities to play regularly if others had not moved on to other situations, yet, once given the chance, their gifting has shone through. I believe that sometimes, as in David's case, those opportunities were engineered by God.

It is important to provide feedback to inexperienced people. They will be desperate to know how they have done. It is important to provide them with both encouragement and points for improvement for the future.

David prays for God to fulfil his promise

(2 Samuel 7:25)

Even though David's vision will not be fulfilled until after his death he prays that God will fulfil his promise.

David committed himself to making succession a success

It is one thing to allow someone else to succeed you – it is another to do everything you can to make the transition successful. We can contrast David's support of Solomon with British political life, where sometimes the outgoing leader of a party has been less than helpful in comments they have made concerning their successor!

David's commitment to Solomon's success is demonstrated in 1 Chronicles 28 and 29. David gathers all the officials and commanders within Israel and his speech has the following features:

- *David endorses both the project and Solomon's leadership* (1 Chronicles 28:2-7). By doing this the people are clear that it is the will of God for Solomon to build the temple, not David. This also gives the people a sense of continuity of vision and purpose.
- *David confirms that Solomon has been chosen by God* for the task – that this is not just 'natural' succession, but ordained by the Lord (28:5-7).

- *David provided practical help and advice* for the project (28:11-17). Solomon would have found practical advice useful from David's experience, but what David offers is superior to this: it is insight from the Spirit of God. This would have been of enormous benefit to Solomon.

- *David gave Solomon personal counsel* (28:9-10). It would have been easy for Solomon to focus exclusively on successfully achieving the task of building the temple. David, however, helpfully reminds him of the inner life – the need to walk before God in integrity. He also reminds him of the Lord's calling upon his life.

- *David recognised Solomon's inexperience.* He emphasised to the people that Solomon needed time to grow into his role (29:1). When there is succession the person taking over is obviously not as experienced as the person they are succeeding. It is inevitable, therefore, that they will make mistakes. This is not because they are not gifted or up to the job: much wisdom comes from experience, some of which can only be gained by doing things wrong initially! David does not undermine Solomon's gifting or calling, but prepares the people for the fact that Solomon may initially make some errors of judgement.

- *David sets an example*
  - By giving from his personal wealth towards the project (29:3-5). David indicates his commitment by sacrificially donating his own gold and silver to facilitate the building work. This provokes others to give generously.
  - In worship (29:10-18). David has been an example in this area for many years – and continues to be so.
  - David prayed for Solomon's success (29:19). It is tempting when someone takes over from you to want them to be successful – but not as successful as you were! God's desire is for us to have the same attitude as Jesus who said that we would do greater things than him, or of

John the Baptist who was content to 'decrease' so that Jesus' ministry would increase.

The result of David's support is that the people acknowledge Solomon as king (29:22). They did not make Solomon king – God had already done this – but they acknowledged what God had already done.

Ultimately, we see that the Lord raises up Solomon (29:25) and the succession is ensured.

Succession is a test of character. God's desire is for us to be wholehearted in enabling others to succeed us so that God's work can continue and that our churches are served continually.

Succession may not be planned

The story of this planned succession concerns a situation where David must have been aware that his own time as king was drawing to a close. I would assume that the fact that he would be succeeded was not a surprise to him! This contrasts with another episode in David's life.

Before David came on the scene, all of Israel would have expected Jonathan to succeed Saul his father as king. Jonathan was a brave and mighty warrior, who, together with his armour bearer, takes on and defeats at least twenty Philistines (1 Samuel 14:4-14) with a remarkable combination of faith and courage: 'Perhaps the Lord will act on our behalf. Nothing can hinder the Lord from saving, whether by many or by few' (verse 6). Furthermore, he does not appear to have inherited the character weaknesses of his father.

Yet David dramatically emerges as God's anointed leader of his people. While Saul became jealous of David and sought to take his life, Jonathan displayed a very different attitude:

> Jonathan made a covenant with David because he loved him as himself. Jonathan took off the robe he was wear-ing and gave it to David, along with his tunic, and even his sword, his bow and his belt. *1 Samuel 18:3-4*

Jonathan later warns David of Saul's desire to kill him and speaks well of David to his father. He helps David 'to find strength in God' by speaking words of faith to David and prophesies David's succession as king instead of himself: 'Don't be afraid. My father Saul will not lay a hand on you. You shall be king over Israel, and I will be second to you' (1 Samuel 23:16-17).

Jonathan's attitude is astonishing. Instead of hindering someone who was a threat to his succession he chooses to bless David by giving him his possessions. The gift of a robe, tunic and belt would have helped David, the shepherd boy, fit in at Saul's court; the sword and bow would have equipped David for future battles.

What is your reaction when someone arrives in your church who is clearly gifted on the instrument that you play? It is tempting to have a 'Saul' attitude. Saul looked good (he 'has slain his thousands') until David showed up (who has 'slain his tens of thousands'). You may not be throwing spears at them, but you'd certainly rather that they weren't there! Your playing doesn't look quite so accomplished now they've arrived!

But God wants us to have the attitude of a 'Jonathan': someone who not only accepts the newcomer but also seeks to bless them and to equip them – even if they will ultimately take our place and restrict our own ministry opportunities! I would not be surprised if you find this immensely challenging – I certainly do! However, it is at times like these that we have to remember that it is God who is observing, 'looking on the heart'. While we can give the outward appearance of accepting the 'David' in our midst, God sees how we react in our heart. But he is there not to condemn but to help us through these times and, if we act and think in a way that pleases him, we can be certain that he will bless us.

Conclusion

It is hard to acknowledge that our own season of ministry in one sphere will at some point come to an end, even if we then serve the Lord in another field, perhaps in another location. However, this is the natural, biblical pattern. God's desire is that we will hold our ministries lightly and be looking to train others to succeed us.

I have so far found that all of those I have sought to train have, after a season with us, moved to other churches, sometimes to start new churches, and God has used them. This is another way that we can see the Lord's work expand. But ultimately the time will come when someone will take over my role and I must prepare my heart for that day.

Our visions and ambitions may be fulfilled by others who come after us. Hebrews 11:39, after listing a great many heroes and heroines of faith who gave themselves sacrificially to the Lord, says:

> These were all commended for their faith, yet none of them received what had been promised. God had planned something better for us so that only together with us would they be made perfect.

God's will is not for us to accomplish everything ourselves, but to be part of a wider team of people, perhaps across churches, countries, and even centuries, who together achieve the purposes of God. Our own part is incomplete: it is only with others that the work can be accomplished.

Points to remember

- *David's desire is godly.* Even though he was not the one to achieve it God commends him for having the desire in his heart.
- *Clarity of vision comes through expression – sharing a vision brings developments.*

- *God's plan is for our 'offspring to succeed us'.* Our roles are temporary and it is often God's plan for spiritual 'sons and daughters' to take our place. We should plan for and disciple those who may take our place.
- *David committed himself to making succession a success.* He did this by:
  - endorsing both the project and Solomon's leadership
  - providing practical help and advice
  - setting an example
  - praying for Solomon's success.
- *When God brings along a successor it is a test whether our attitude will be like Saul's, or like Jonathan's.*

Questions for personal application

1. Solomon says, 'My father David had it in his heart to build a temple.' What desires do you have in your heart?

2. Are there any occasions in your life where you handed over ministry in the church to someone else?

3. Is there anyone in your church who has the gifting to be able to step into your current role in your church?

4. If so, how can you develop them to be able to do so?

5. If God told you today to lay down your role to let someone else step in, what emotions would you experience? Would you find it difficult to step aside? How can you deal with these emotions?

CHAPTER 11

The end? (2 Samuel 23)

The last words of David

These are the last words of David:

> The oracle of David son of Jesse, the oracle of the man
>   exalted by the Most High,
> the man anointed by the God of Jacob, Israel's singer of
>   songs:
>
> The Spirit of the Lord spoke through me; his word was
>   on my tongue.
> The God of Israel spoke, the Rock of Israel said to me:
> 'When one rules over men in righteousness, when he
>   rules in the fear of God,
> he is like the light of morning at sunrise on a cloudless
>   morning,
> like the brightness after rain that brings the grass from
>   the earth.'
>
> Is not my house right with God? Has he not made with
>   me an everlasting covenant,
> arranged and secured in every part?
> Will he not bring to fruition my salvation and grant me
>   my every desire?
> But evil men are all to be cast aside like thorns, which
>   are not gathered with the hand.
> Whoever touches thorns uses a tool of iron or the shaft
>   of a spear;
> they are burned up where they lie.

This passage is described as 'the last words of David'. They are probably his last poetic testimony, rather than necessarily his last ever words. Nevertheless, they serve as the epitaph by which David wished to be remembered.

All things on earth come to an end. We are mortal and, as the apostle Paul writes 'outwardly we are wasting away' (2 Corinthians 4:16). Our lives and our ministries will cease.

At such times, people tend to focus only on those things that are most important. It is said that no one on their deathbed ever wishes they had put more hours in at the office! What does David remember?

Exalted and anointed by God

Verses 2 and 3 indicate that David does not take pride in what he has achieved. Rather, he acknowledges that anything accomplished by him was due to the fact that God gave him gifts and raised him up within Israel. Whatever we achieve in life is due to God – it is he who gives us the gifts and creates the circumstances in which we can exercise them. 'From him . . . and to him are all things' (Romans 11:36). 'Every good and perfect gift is from above' (James 1:17). There is nothing of ourselves we can take pride in. 'Let him who boasts boast in the Lord' (2 Corinthians 10:17).

'Israel's singer of songs'

David could have chosen to describe himself as a great king, a military hero, a supremely gifted musician and songwriter. Instead he shows humility by describing himself just as a 'singer of songs'. I believe that ultimately he saw himself, first and foremost, as a worshipper. His primary reason for existence was to give glory to the Lord.

Ultimately, the story of David is a tale of two people – David and his God. How God exalted David, protected him, provided for him, guided him, and above all, loved him. How David sought after his God and yearned to know him, to follow him and to be like him. Ultimately, whatever you achieve in your life, your story is about you and God. When we 'appear before the judgment seat of Christ' (2 Corinthians 5:10) we will not be judged by how many meetings we have played at or how good our singing was, but rather by our obedience to what the Lord asked us to do: whether we were faithful in the small things and the greater things; whether we loved the Lord with all our heart, mind, soul and strength; whether we loved our neighbour as ourselves. And if these are the areas we will be judged on, these are what we should concentrate on.

David's satisfaction and contentment comes from obedience (2 Samuel 23:3-4)

Some, at the end of their lives, might express dissatisfaction. It is worth remembering that while David had many blessings he also experienced suffering. Unjust treatment at the hands of Saul meant he spent much time in hiding and in exile. He could have been bitter over this. The rebellion of his own son, Absalom, could have led him to feel resentment and hurt. He could still have felt guilty over his affair with Bathsheba and the murder of Uriah. David's contentment lies in the fact that, generally, he ruled 'over men in righteousness . . . in the fear of God'. When we are obedient to the Lord this brings peace. When we know that we have fulfilled what he has entrusted to us, even though we may have failed at times, this brings lasting contentment.

David took pleasure that his house was 'right with God' (verse 5). It was not just his own relationship with God that was right, but, at this stage, Solomon had not yet drifted from paths of righteousness, snared by wealth and his many foreign wives. Our responsibility is not limited to our own relationship with God, but to do all that we can to ensure that our 'house' is right with God. We must not be so consumed by our musical gifts and callings that we neglect our spouse and children, but instead devote ourselves to them, not least in helping them in their relationship with the Lord.

David knew his desires would be fulfilled (2 Samuel 23:5)

From a mortal perspective verse 5 appears strange – how could God grant David his every desire if he was dying? Of course, David understood that death was not the end. In Psalm 16 he says, 'you have made known to me the path of life; you will fill me with joy in your presence, with eternal pleasures at your right hand' (verse 11). David knew that fulfilment was to come.

Life will always be, to a certain extent, unfulfilling. Aside from persecution and suffering, there may be a sense of frustration about ministry. This will probably be exacerbated in the area where our gifting lies. Evangelists must be frustrated that not all the earth has as yet heard the gospel and millions do not yet acknowledge Jesus as Lord. Pastors are dismayed when church members do not always grow to become mature in Christ and may even backslide. As worship leaders and musicians we may be disappointed that we do not experience the presence of God as powerfully as described in some passages of Scripture. We may also be frustrated if worship is not the priority in our church that we think it should be.

The wonderful news for every Christian is that on the final day everyone will acknowledge Jesus to be Lord. When we see him we shall be like him, and we shall worship the Lord forever in a dimension of praise and adoration that we have not yet experienced. As he comes again in majesty we will see everything subject to his will.

When worship at our church is not going as well as I'd like it to I remind myself of this – that one day God will 'bring to fruition my salvation and grant me my every desire'.

What is David remembered for?

Looking back at the end of David's life it is tempting to define him by his achievements. After all, it's a great story! He defeated Goliath, survived Saul's attempts on his life and ultimately became a glorious king. Yet in his own epitaph it is clear that David did not define himself by his exploits. It is as if the external events of his life are secondary to something else – the relationship he had with the Lord. I'd like to summarise David's life in two quotations by the apostle Paul in Acts 13:

> For when David had served God's purpose in his own generation, he fell asleep; he was buried with his fathers and his body decayed. *Acts 13:36*

David served the purpose of God in his generation. Despite sin and some other failures in his life, this is how he was remembered. Our gifting may never be as great as David's. We may not be 'exalted' to the profile and have the same opportunities to lead God's people, to write songs and to initiate projects in the way David did. However, each of us can serve the purpose of God in our generation within the scope of our gifts and our circumstances. If we are faithful to what we have been entrusted with, the Lord will say to us, 'Well done, good and faithful servant' (Matthew 25:21).

The second quote says:

> After removing Saul, he [God] made David their king. He testified concerning him: 'I have found David son of Jesse *a man after my own heart*; he will do everything I want him to do.' *Acts 13:22*

Many men in David's position would have made being king their primary focus. Instead, David's preoccupation was the King of kings. He longed to know God more, to serve him, to follow him and to be like him. This is why God bestows such a tremendous accolade upon him. If we seek after the Lord himself and his kingdom we, too, can be known as those who are 'after God's own heart'.

Much of this book has, necessarily, focused on externals. We have looked at how to build a worship team, run rehearsals, lead worship and write songs. These are necessary skills for those involved in worship. But there is a danger that we can become preoccupied *with* worship. We must instead ensure that our attention is *primarily on the object of our worship*, the King of Glory, Jesus Christ.

Join with me in aiming to be those who are 'after God's own heart', running after him all our lives, knowing that one day we will see him face to face. We will then be able to enjoy him forever, in a worship time with no limits that will give us unimaginable joy as we see Jesus given the praise, the honour and the glory he so richly deserves. Come soon, Lord Jesus.

Points to remember

- *'Israel's singer of songs'.* David chose to describe himself as a worshipper rather than as a great king. Ultimately our lives are about two people – ourselves and God – rather than any achievements or roles we have in our lives.

- *David knew his desires would be fulfilled in eternity.* We can look forward to the fulfilment of God's word and our own desires in heaven.

- *David is remembered as, first, 'serving the purposes of God in his generation'.* We will be judged on our obedience to the Lord's commands and our faithfulness in the tasks he has entrusted us with.

- *David is remembered as, second, being a 'man after God's own heart',* who passionately sought after his Lord. If we seek him and his kingdom this is how we can be remembered, too.

Questions for personal application

1. What gifts has God given you to serve in the church?

2. Can you see occasions in your life when God has 'exalted and anointed' you to perform particular tasks for him?

3. What areas in church life across the nation do you feel frustrated about?

4. What does Scripture say about what will happen to these areas when Jesus returns?

5. Spend a few moments writing your own epitaph. How would you like to be remembered?

Leading worship: Practical tips
The balloon ride

This section sets out some advice on the more practical aspects of leading worship, that didn't fit readily into chapters on David.

I often think of worship as being like a balloon ride. Before you get in the balloon, your perspective is limited – you can only see the things immediately around you. These can seem very big. But as the balloon takes off your perspective changes. As you rise, the situation you were in begins to look smaller compared with the wider countryside that has come into view. You can now see a lot of things you couldn't see before. After your balloon ride you land refreshed and exhilarated, having viewed things from a different perspective.

When we come to worship our perspective is limited. Our day-to-day situations and problems may appear to be very large, even insurmountable. Sometimes they can weigh heavily on our hearts.

But as we begin to worship the almighty, all-knowing God our perspective changes. We are reminded that he is in control, that ultimately everything is under his feet and that our problems, which seemed so big, now seem smaller compared with this all-powerful God. As we think about the Lord – who he is and what he has done – and as we begin to take our eyes off ourselves and fix our eyes on Jesus, it's as if we're being lifted up. The situations and circumstances that seemed so big, are put in their rightful perspective as we look at things from God's eternal, heavenly viewpoint. When the worship time finishes our problems have not been resolved, but our perspective on them has been changed.

To continue this analogy further, in leading worship we will be:

- taking off
- gaining altitude
- making a soft landing.

Taking off

In order to get off the ground we need some hot air in the balloon. What is spiritual 'hot air'? In John chapter 4 Jesus says that 'God is spirit and his worshippers must worship in spirit and truth.' I believe that, to get our worship off the ground, we need both spirit and truth.

Preparation

The first way we can get hot air into the balloon is before the meeting itself – in our preparation. Like David drawing aside to the stream to get his weapons before he fought Goliath, we need to spend time preparing.

In Chapters 3 and 5 I talked about the well and how I prepare a theme and also a list of songs. Everyone will find what works best for them. However, it is essential to draw aside to seek the Lord.

Introduction to worship

It is helpful to introduce the theme to the worship time.

I have heard Graham Kendrick say that while there are literally hundreds (probably thousands) of reasons to worship God, it is helpful to give people a reason to worship him at the beginning of a meeting. When your congregation arrives at the meeting, having perhaps rushed to get children ready, found somewhere to park and a seat in the meeting, they may not feel immediately attuned to seeking the presence of God! If we draw their attention to, say, an aspect of God's character, or something he has done, it helps them to focus on him.

I will therefore read a few words of Scripture and briefly summarise them. Scripture is particularly helpful as an introduction as it injects the 'hot air' of truth into the balloon. It is tempting, particularly if you feel inspired, to give a 'sermonette' with several points, but I believe that all people need is a 'soundbite' – a few short words to start them off. If you speak for much more than one minute it is probably too long.

At the beginning of meetings you may find that your congregation is not very disciplined about paying attention. People are still arriving, chatting to their friends or reading notice sheets. I used to find this frustrating – I would be sharing a Scripture that I felt was significant and people would not be listening! To avoid this, we now play one song to gather everyone together and then give an introduction after this.

Spirit and truth in song selection

Some worship songs have more truth in them than others! If I want to use a song that is a bit lightweight lyrically I will balance it with songs that contain plenty of scripturally based images and references. It is harder to define how much 'Spirit' is in a song, but some songs do have an 'anointing' on them, and seem to be able to 'lift' the congregation. A good, recent example is 'Here I Am (Majesty)' by Delirious which has a clear anointing. One difficulty with such songs is, because of their success in worship times, they can be over-used. The congregation then becomes over-familiar with them, and they lose their impact. We need to handle them with care!

You will have spent time preparing the worship time beforehand, and perhaps praying and worshipping together with your band before the meeting. You will hopefully find that you are very ready to praise God wholeheartedly – and this is a great place to be! However, your congregation may be a little behind you and can sometimes take a few minutes before they 'warm up'. Try to lead them gently from where they are to where you want them to be, mindful that you have a 'head start' on them.

Gaining altitude – allowing the Holy Spirit to use other people to put air into the balloon

In trying to get the balloon further off the ground we need some more hot air. The Bible shows us clearly that contributions from the congregation help. I have already mentioned these in Chapter 5.

The New Testament teaching is clear:

- The Holy Spirit gives gifts to members of the congregation when the church gathers together.
- It is through participation from various members of the body that the church is strengthened.

Contributions are the diesel oil of worship. They can cause worship times to catch fire, but they are also very messy to handle! I have known worship to really take off as a result of contributions, and I have also known them to deflate the worship!

I believe that the first letter to the Corinthians makes it clear that contributions are the biblical pattern for worship. The only reason I can see to move away from this model is where circumstances make it impractical, such as:

- *Very large meetings,* where it isn't practical to open up the opportunity to contribute to everyone in the meeting. However, a number of leaders and/or others could be present on a platform where they could speak or sing into a microphone so that even in this sort of situation there can be contributions.
- *At a meeting with people from a number of different types of churches.* I have not found this to be practical because people

may feel unfamiliar with worshipping together and because people from such different backgrounds will be used to different expressions of worship.

Apart from these exceptions I believe that worship leaders need to create an environment in which the body of Christ can bring spiritual gifts and other contributions to the meeting. Jesus' body is made up of many parts – not just one. If we want the Holy Spirit to anoint the worship we have to give opportunity for him to use the body of Christ.

This is where it gets a little frightening for the worship leader – it's much easier to sing one song after another, effectively keeping control of the worship time.

If your church's worship times do not currently have members of the congregation participating, then it is something that can only be introduced with the consent of your church leadership. It is helpful for your church leadership to provide teaching into this area because there can be difficulties.

You will have gathered from all I have said that I believe passionately in the biblical basis and the power of contributions to lift up the 'balloon' of worship. I would greatly encourage people to speak out what they believe God is saying to them. If we make a mistake the church is a family and we should be gracious to each other. However, there are a couple of ways in which our worship times can be enhanced:

- the timing of contributions
- the length of contributions.

The timing of contributions

To return to our theme of the balloon ride, some contributions help us to 'take off', others help us to come back down to earth and focus on applying what God has said to our situations. Often, Christians bring contributions but they do not bring them at the best time in the meeting.

Let's imagine an example. A member of your church, 'Fred', is very ill in hospital. Naturally, everyone at your housegroup meeting is concerned and wants to pray for Fred, that God will heal him and comfort his family at this difficult time. You can imagine that during the worship, after your first song, someone can't contain themselves and prays for Fred. While no real harm has been done, in the context of the balloon ride we haven't gained any altitude yet – Fred's situation still seems to loom large for all of us. But if we carry on worshipping the Lord for a while and remind ourselves of his greatness and his power and pray for Fred at the end of the worship our perspective will have been changed. We can see that the all-powerful, all-loving God is in control of this and every other circumstance. We can then pray for Fred at the end, 'coming down to land' full of faith for Fred's situation now that our perspective has been changed. It may be worth remembering Philippians chapter 4 where Paul encourages the Philippians to rejoice in the Lord, then to present their requests to God and then to receive God's peace. Praise is a great prelude to prayer!

The same is true where we are concerned about evangelism. Of course, we are all desperate to see God move among our neighbours, friends and family members who have not yet come to a saving knowledge of the Lord. But if we pray for them too early in the worship time, before we have really had an opportunity to experience God's perspective, our balloon ride will be very short and we will not be in a place of faith.

I believe passionately that it is biblical to have prophetic* words during worship times; however, their impact is enhanced if we bring them at an appropriate time. Some prophetic words, that remind us of God's majesty and glory and what he has done for us, stir us on to worship the Lord

---

* I am not limiting this definition of 'prophetic' to foretelling the future. For a definition of prophecy please see Chapter 8 on prophetic worship.

and make the balloon rise. However, words that give specific direction to the church (e.g. 'you are moving into a season when you need to reach out more into the community') fit better at the end of the worship time, when we are focusing back on our situations, having reminded ourselves of who God is. I mentioned in Chapter 5 the model of Psalm 95, in which a prophetic word came after both joyful praise and reflective worship and I believe that this model suits most worship times.

When we as individuals believe we have received a word from the Lord we can feel so stirred up we feel like we will burst if we don't speak it out! We can also be so nervous that our sense of timing goes awry! However, if people say that they couldn't hold back their prophetic word then they are adopting an unbiblical position! 1 Corinthians 14:32 says, 'The spirits of prophets are subject to the control of prophets.' We help our churches if we learn to wait for the opportune time.

I have drawn up a table with some ideas of when contributions may be most suitable in a worship time.

Taking off	Coming back to land
Prayer (Thanksgiving)	Prayer (Intercession)
Reading Scripture (Who God is and what he has done – e.g. *'Sing to the Lord a new song, for he has done marvellous things'*, Psalm 98)	Reading Scripture (Application – e.g. *'Be transformed by the renewing of your mind'*)
Songs extolling God (Who God is and what he has done) Songs exhorting the people to worship God	Songs responding to God, or expressing how the empowered church will affect the nation
Tongues and Interpretations	Words of knowledge
Prophecy (Who God is and what he has done)	Prophecy (Application and direction)

Tongues are *to* God, not from God to man

1 Corinthians 14:2 says, 'For anyone who speaks in a tongue does not speak to men but to God.' When someone speaks in a tongue in a meeting they are speaking to God. This means that the interpretation should be from man to God, e.g. 'Lord, my heart pants for you like the deer pants for the water' rather than as a prophecy from God to man 'I want your heart to pant for me like a deer after water.'*

Length of contributions

The other common area in which contributions can 'deflate the balloon' is when they go on too long. You can sense the congregation, which had been engaged in worshipping the Lord, beginning to switch off. Sometimes the person bringing the contribution started off well, but has not known when to stop.

When we speak out in a meeting we may feel that we have not adequately communicated what we wanted to say. It is tempting to keep going in an effort to ensure that our message is understood, when in fact everyone else has grasped the point clearly right at the beginning.

We can also sometimes allow the response (or lack of it) from others to dictate the length of our contribution. If we are in an environment where people give vocal affirmation ('Amen', 'Yes Lord') if they agree, we may be tempted to keep going if it is clear that people are with us in our prayer or song, when it is better to leave everyone wanting more, rather than wanting us to stop! I have heard some people bring contributions that have got the whole congregation with them, clearly injecting air into the balloon: if they stopped at that point they would have given us significant 'lift'. Unfortunately they have continued and ultimately deflated the meeting!

---

* I am indebted to Phil Rogers for this example, taken from *Receiving the Holy Spirit and His Gifts*, Terry Virgo and Phil Rogers, Word Books/Frontier Publishing International, 1991.

On the other hand, if we get no response from others we can feel embarrassed that we have spoken out, so we keep going in the hope of redeeming ourselves! In fact, we should not measure the quality of our contributions by people's responses. People may be quiet because they are listening intently. When the woman broke the alabaster jar and poured perfume on Jesus' feet she drew criticism for her contribution from all except Jesus, yet Jesus made it clear that her offering was acceptable to him. When the widow offered her mite she was not praised by others, but Jesus made it clear that he valued what she had given.

Contributions in different directions!

It may well happen that you are leading worship on a particular theme and then someone in the congregation brings a contribution on a different subject. You then have to make a decision – to go with their theme, or to stick with what you have already prepared.

Obviously if there is a strong favourable reaction from *the congregation* to what the person has said I would probably change direction. Similarly, if there is little response from the congregation then I will stick with my original theme.

However, you have to make a judgement at the time. Remember that you have the Holy Spirit with you. Talk to him. I often find he tells me the next step, perhaps only at the last moment! We also have to overcome the 'inertia' factor – it's easier and more comfortable to stick with the songs we've prepared, rather than having to think on our feet! You could also ask a member of your leadership team what they think. It is useful if they aren't standing too far away from you when you are leading, as they are a very helpful sounding board.

Responding to prophetic words

When prophecies are brought in our churches it is important that we give them proper consideration. Scripture says, 'Two or three prophets should speak, and the others should weigh carefully what is said' (1 Corinthians 14:29). It may be that your leadership wants to lead people in a response, in which case we need to step back, even if we're itching to do another song! However, often they may leave it to the worship leader to take the meeting forward. These are the sort of things I might do:

- Lead people in a prayer of response.

- Encourage people to pray (people raising their voices together, all praying prayers individually but at the same time [Acts 4:24]).

- Have a few moments' silence to reflect on what has been said. It is useful to say that this is what you're doing, or someone else will speak!

- Sing a song that directly follows from the thrust of the prophetic words. For example, if the word is that God is looking for us to be more devoted to him, it would be appropriate to sing a song that expressed our desire to follow him. I would often say a couple of sentences to summarise what has been said, and encourage people to sing the song as a response.

Scripture states that 'two or three prophets should speak, and the others should weigh carefully what is said.' I have sometimes been at meetings where there are five or six prophecies one after another. The trouble with this is that the congregation can feel overloaded with information and then the impact of the first couple of prophecies is lost. I would, therefore, always encourage a response after two or three prophecies. Hopefully there will be an opportunity later for others to speak. However, Scripture also compares the word of the Lord to 'rain and snow' in Isaiah 55:10. Sometimes in a meeting many people will have prophetic words that are essentially the same – they are different drops of rain, but the same shower! It may be that we don't need all six or seven people to speak in order to hear the Lord's message to us. God has given several people a similar message to encourage them, and the rest of the congregation, that many people received the same message – there was a unity among the congregation about the word God had for us.

Managing contributions

As I said earlier, contributions are like diesel oil – they can ignite and power the meeting, but they can also be very messy. In more than twenty years of going to Christian meetings I have heard very few contributions that were totally unscriptural. When these do come they probably need to be publicly corrected; however, I think our church leadership would do this, rather than the worship leader. I have, however, heard some that weren't that helpful. If this happens I try to 'pick up the pieces' by perhaps praying in a way that draws something from what has just been said, but to re-direct it onto the theme, and to quote some Scripture so that we get back onto a firm foundation.

Participation for all?

1 Corinthians 14:26 says that 'everyone' has a contribution to bring. It is feasible in a small setting, such as a home group, for each member to say something, However, as a matter of practicality, if a church meeting gets significantly larger than this then not everyone can contribute.* Our church meetings have approximately three hundred people and if everyone spoke for just thirty seconds we'd be in for a very long worship time! However, I want everyone to feel that they could participate. I am, therefore, looking for ways in which people can be active in participating in other ways, rather than just in singing songs. These might include:

---

* I believe that the meaning of 1 Corinthians 14:26 is that each member could bring a contribution – not that every person has to say something for the Scripture to be fulfilled!

- reading a psalm or other passage of Scripture together
- singing – in tongues, or I may spontaneously come up with some words and a melody that I will ask people to sing
- encouraging people to respond with their bodies – raising hands, clapping, dancing, kneeling.

Making a soft landing

Near the end of the worship we need to think about 'landing'. How do we conclude the worship in such a way that it helps us to get ready to face the outside world again but still keeping our eyes fixed upon Jesus, in the light of seeing God's heavenly perspective?

There can be a strong temptation to focus on our individual problems. If we do this then the end of the worship time can seem inward looking. It may be better to focus outward – to express something of God's perspective and love for the world, so that we conclude our worship conscious that we are on a mission.

This can be done by praying, thanking God for what he's said to us, and summarising this within the prayer. Another way would be to sing a song that was focused on God's desire to reach the unchurched, and his triumphant return. At certain times it may be appropriate to have a time of ministering to each other by praying, getting into groups of two or three and praying for each other.

'Character' questions

As a practical application of Chapter 1 (on character) here are a few light-hearted questions to ask yourself as a musician. Be honest with yourself! It's good, although painful, to test your attitudes!

1. Someone joins the church who plays the same instrument as you. They make their debut at playing one Sunday morning. After the meeting everyone is talking about how 'wonderful' their playing was – some people even make a point of telling *you* this! Do you:
   a. smile sweetly, but seethe inwardly?
   b. draw attention to some minor deficiency or mistake they made?
   c. go home and practise all week in a (vain) attempt to regain 'top spot'?
   d. do none of the above?

2. You are practising during the week on your own and you come up with what you think is a brilliant part for your instrument in a worship song. When you play it in the rehearsal the musicians' leader says he/she doesn't think it fits. Do you:
   a. say, 'That's never stopped you before'?
   b. try to rally other people in the group to your support?
   c. when the song is used in the worship time just play the part anyway?
   d. do none of the above?

3. You have been asked to lead worship and you have spent hours praying about it and preparing. Early on the Sunday morning your pastor rings you and apologises, but says that because there are many other things happening that morning he only wants two songs/10 minutes' worship. Do you:
   a. argue the point with him?
   b. pray that the Spirit falls on the congregation after the first song – just to prove him wrong?
   c. sulk?
   d. refuse ever to lead worship again?
   e. at the end of the second song lead the congregation into singing in the Spirit in an attempt to prolong the worship as much as possible, then say 'the Spirit led us that way'?
   f. change your plans and get 100 per cent behind what your pastor is trying to achieve?

4. It's a Sunday morning and you play the best you've ever played. You really flowed, and felt truly anointed. When you sit down your best friend says they couldn't hear you at all through the PA. Do you:
   a. find the PA man and 'lay hands' on him – preferably on his throat?
   b. refuse to play again – what's the point?
   c. make *sure* that next week you're the loudest?
   d. say you don't really care 'it's all for an audience of one', but really you do?
   e. see if you can help the PA team on weeks you aren't playing to see what it's like to mix from their perspective?

5. Your church is suddenly blessed with a number of new musicians joining. The musicians' leader wants to introduce them into the band and asks if you would mind playing less frequently than you currently do. Do you:
   a. argue with the musicians' leader – who are these 'Johnny come latelys', anyway?

b. find a church leader and complain?

c. start looking for another church?

d. invite one of the new musicians round, befriend them and pray for them?

Song Assessment Sheet*

Here are some questions to ask when assessing a new song for corporate worship:

1. What is the theme of the song?

2. What does the song actually teach?

3. Are there any obscure phrases in the song where the meaning might be unclear to people?

4. Does the song reinforce biblical teaching – or undermine it?

5. Is the song God-centred, or man-centred?

6. Does the song focus primarily on objective truth or subjective feelings and experiences?

7. Is the song easy for a congregation to sing (e.g. range, timing, intervals between notes)?

8. Any other good or bad points about the song?

9. Where would you use it during corporate worship? (Does the song fit thematically in many times of worship? Would you play the song near the beginning, or only towards the end?)

---

* I am indebted to Peter Harwood of Penge Family Church, South East London, for this sheet.